EAT JOY

EAT JOY

STORIES & COMFORT FOOD FROM
31 CELEBRATED WRITERS

Edited by

NATALIE EVE GARRETT

WITH ILLUSTRATIONS BY MERYL ROWIN

NEW YORK

First published in the United States in 2019 by Black Balloon, an imprint of Catapult (catapult.co)

ISBN: 978-1-936787-79-1

Cover design and book illustrations by Meryl Rowin

Book design by Wah-Ming Chang

Catapult titles are distributed to the trade by Publishers Group West

Phone: 866-400-5351

Library of Congress Control Number: 2018967674

Printed in China

10 9 8 7 6 5 4 3 2 1

For Tony, Serafina, Aurelio

&

for you.

CONTENTS

GROWING PAINS

LOSS

HEALING

HOMECOMING

INTRODUCTION

L ooking back on some of the more challenging times in my life, I remember not only the emotions involved, but also the taste. When I was sixteen, for instance, I was repeatedly bedridden with mysterious fevers that raged for months. My memories of that sweaty delirium are inextricably linked to the flavor of apple tarts: glazed apples and creamy custard set in a crisp buttery crust, then covered with toasted almond slices that crumbled onto the sheets with each bite. My mom bought them at a nearby bakery and delivered them to my bedside on particularly dark days. Another memory: a perfectly ripe, juicy cantaloupe—sliced in half, the hollow lusciously filled with blueberries—left in a bowl on the counter on the summer morning that I broke up with my first real boyfriend. I ran down the stairs and escaped into a blast of July heat, teary yet exhilarated, with bits of blueberry still stuck to my teeth. Or the birth of my daughter, and then two years and three months later, my son: soft scrambled eggs, potatoes, and whole wheat toast with butter and raspberry jam; easy, simple foods, eaten for every single hospital meal, and for many meals during the subsequent weeks at home in bed—a dim haze of ice packs, exhaustion, blood, and adoration.

When I embarked on this collection, I hoped to create a feast of stories about making mistakes, summoning strength, getting lost and trying to find a way back. I hungered for compassionate stories that reveled in taste, whether savory, bitter, or sweet—stories that used food as a conduit for unearthing memories. Reaching out to celebrated writers, I asked them to chronicle the hard times—immigration challenges, chronic illness, loss, heartbreak, and more—and the foods that help them make it through. I gathered tips for scavenging, foraging, and scrimping; meditations on eating and friendship and finding comfort in eating alone; the secrets to favorite stress-relieving meals; nourishment in the face of addiction; unusual cravings; tales of troubled relationships with food; healing recipes.

The result: *Eat Joy: Stories & Comfort Food from 31 Celebrated Writers*, an unconventional collection of intimate, in-depth essays with recipes celebrating the foods we eat to get through the dark times in our lives. Each piece grapples with adversity and self-discovery; each acts as a reminder of our resilience. And taste ties the pieces together. Collectively, the book presents a hopeful vision, and it serves up delicious things to eat along the way.

In this book, Diana Abu-Jaber recalls the flight of her Palestinian ancestors from their villages in 1948. Edwidge Danticat finds magic in a simple dish that she eats with her dying father. Melissa Febos confronts Imposter Syndrome; Anthony Doerr feels homesick among humpback whales and bald eagles; Colum McCann shares a profound meditation on grief.

Offering solace, inspiration, and love, *Eat Joy* serves up mouth-watering dishes with a side of restorative joy. May the stories and recipes nourish you too.

NATALIE EVE GARRETT

EAT JOY

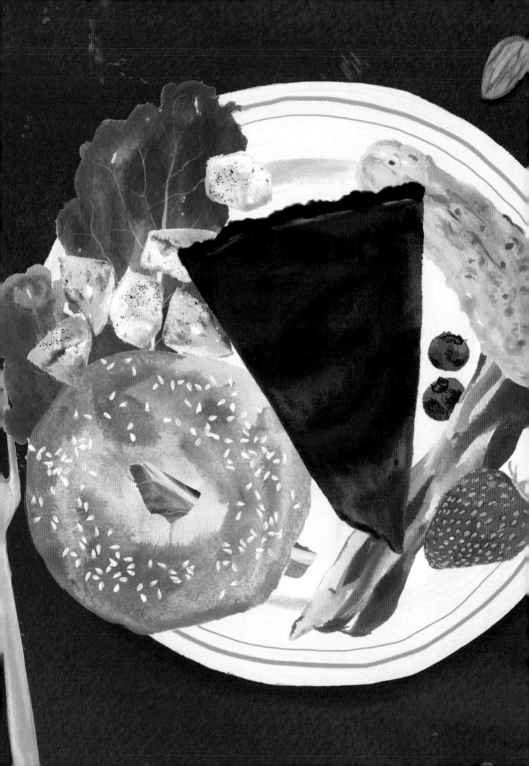

Growing Pains

LEAVES

DIANA ABU-JABER

Diana Abu-Jaber is the author of two memoirs: *Life Without a Recipe*—an Indie Next title—and *The Language of Baklava*, as well as four award-winning novels, including *Birds of Paradise*; *Origin*; *Crescent*; and *Arabian Jazz*. Her YA fantasy novel *SilverWorld* is forthcoming next year. Diana teaches at Portland State University and lives with her husband and daughter in Fort Lauderdale.

They were so hungry. So hungry. They ate the leaves off the trees." That's what my auntie says, describing the flight of the Palestinians from their villages in 1948. "They ate the herbs that grew in the fields—wild thyme and oregano. Za'atar. Just leaves." Aunt Nura is married to my father's cousin Omar. My father's family is Jordanian, from the city of Es-Salt, but Nura grew up across the border in Beit Nabala, in the district of Ramle. She was one of thousands who fled for their lives when the first waves of soldiers arrived. Most left with the clothes on their backs—a few took the time to lock their doors and courtyards and buried or pocketed the iron keys—never to return.

As a child listening to my auntie's stories, I imagined the fleeing villagers also as children, their bare feet and wind-tangled hair. I pictured them as enchanted creatures, like Thumbelina, living on dewdrops and petals, without pasts or futures, aware only of each moment of movement, crossing leafy hillsides to look forward into the wide Jordan Valley, never allowing themselves a backward glance. I imagined other stories for them: that green blossoms fell from the clouds and turned out to be full of honey; that they were saved by pirates on camelback towing ships across the sand. I imagined that they *forgot*, like the children in fairytales do, because forgetting is such a powerful yet close form of magic—cooling and sweet.

My aunt called this flight the *hejira*—which is part escape, part migration, part pilgrimage. It's an important word in Arabic, filled with resonance. The prophet Mohammed's great *hejira*, from Mecca to Medina—both to evade assassins and to bring together his followers—marks the first year of the Islamic calendar. Nura was too young to remember much about the escape, yet she tells this story over and over, as if possessed. Whenever Uncle Omar hears his wife use the word *hejira*, however, he scoffs. "A *hejira*," he says, "has a beginning, middle, and most importantly an end. Your auntie's

has none of these. She's still on the journey."

There have been many times in my life when I've gone on the *hejira*, times that I've traveled thousands of miles to a new school, or job, or for no reason at all, except hope. I've traveled with a single suitcase to my name, lived in a basement apartment with only folding chairs and a cardboard box for furniture. On two occasions of leaving two previous husbands, I took nothing but a toothbrush and a change of clothes. And when I think of these times, perhaps it's a sign of being a lucky and spoiled American, but I mainly recall a feeling of freedom, of bursting through obstacles.

At those times when I've struggled to hang on, to be safe, to control this job or that relationship, to buy or keep more than I needed, I've felt a heaviness that tells me I've gone down the wrong path. I prefer the solace of cooking, which can offer both freedom and comfort. Like my exiled auntie who prepared the dishes of her lost childhood, whenever I've gone on *hejira*, I've found myself back in spice markets and import stores and falafel stands. I wander into musty shops and inhale olives brining in their barrels, bring my nose close to bright pyramids of saffron and cumin and sumac and sesame. I carry home bags filled with herbs, sprinkle spoonfuls of za'atar on my eggs and toast and soup. The spices bring back memory—the oldest, shining memories, that came long before any painful new mistakes and reversals.

Children of immigrants know it is terribly difficult to try to hang on not only to our own memories but to those of our parents. What if I don't make the shish kabob exactly the way my father did? Am I allowed to tamper with his stuffed grape leaves—especially now that his generation is leaving us? If I take such risks, will anything be left? What may be dared and what must be preserved?

These days, I'm notice couscous and hummus and baba ghanouj—such classic Arab dishes—rebranded as *Israeli* on labels and menus. The problem isn't one of sharing—generosity is practically a sacrament in the Arab world—but of cultural erasure. Each time I see this form of renaming, it's as if my aunt lost not only her childhood house, but the things that made it home—all the feasts and lunches, her pistachio cookies, chicken *msukken*, and smoked bulgur and tabbouleh salad, dishes handed down from her mother's grandmother, extending into the roots of the olive orchards and date palms.

Reportedly, the Israelis have outlawed the picking of herbs like za'atar and thyme, contending

> " Cooking is *hejira* — departure & return. If you never strike out or take chances, you may become imprisoned; if you run too far, you may get lost."
>
> —Diana Abu-Jaber

that such plants are endangered, and encouraging its cultivation in gardens instead. But wild za'atar is said to be the miraculous herb that fed the Palestinians, an ingredient at the heart of their food and identity for ages. There are no substitutes.

INCREASINGLY, I'VE COME TO understand that there are many different layers to a home—a landscape, a house, a name. All things alter through time, and not everything has to be preserved in its historical perfection. I recognize *home* in the faces around me, in memory and imagination. I find it in taste and scent, and I find it is much improved when it's shared.

Cooking is *hejíra*—departure and return. If you never strike out or take chances, you may become imprisoned; if you run too far, you may get lost. There is a balance between tradition and creativity, the honey and the bitter herbs. I laugh each time I think of the stuffed grape leaves my American brother-in-law prepared for my father: they had a vegetarian filling, made with raisins in the rice instead of ground lamb. Dad politely ate one, but when my brother-in-law left the room, Dad rolled his eyes, laughed, and said, "*Ya meskeen!*" Oh the poor guy!

They're both gone now, but the memory of the raisin grape leaves lives on in family lore. To be honest, I thought those grape leaves were pretty good: they just weren't the way Dad made them.

The taste of home includes the touch of the first cook—their recipe, their taste. It transcends notions of deliciousness; this kind of "delicious" contains the past itself, its continuity, its repetition, the satisfaction of performing, once again, the ritual: these ingredients, this preparation, this presentation. It tells us we are connected to something larger than ourselves, something older, something like a home. And then, having eaten, we get to leave it again.

Za'atar bi Zayt

Different regions have different versions of za'atar. Usually the blend will contain wild za'atar—sometimes called wild hyssop—as well as some combination of oregano, thyme, sumac, and sesame seeds. It comes in different colors and blends—I prefer those from Palestine, Jordan, Syria, and Lebanon. Cooks will sprinkle it on everything from dips to sandwiches or use it as a spice rub. One of my favorite ways to roast chicken is to first douse it in za'atar. But for basic comfort, I think the simple dish of za'atar, lebeneh, and oil is best.

big scoop of lebeneh	small heap of za'atar
drizzle or three of good olive oil	fresh loaf of pita bread, cut into triangles

These days, many stores carry containers of lebeneh, but it's very easy to make. Simply place a container of plain, full-fat yogurt into a lined coffee filter or several layers of paper towels inside a mesh strainer over a bowl. Overnight, the liquid will drain out. Discard. The remaining yogurt will have thickened into a creamy, mild dip.

Place the lebeneh in a bowl; make a trough in the yogurt with the back of a spoon.

Drizzle oil liberally over the trough. Sprinkle with za'atar. Dip in with pita or chopped-up crudités.

Serves about two, depending on appetite.

COMFORT WITH EGGS

LAURA VAN DEN BERG

Laura van den Berg is the author of the novel *Find Me* and two story collections, *What the World Will Look Like When All the Water Leaves Us* and *The Isle of Youth*. Her honors include the Bard Fiction Prize, the Rosenthal Family Foundation Award from the American Academy of Arts and Letters, a Pushcart Prize, an O. Henry Award, and fellowships from the MacDowell Colony and the Civitella Ranieri Foundation. Laura is a Briggs-Copeland Lecturer in Fiction at Harvard University and lives in Cambridge with her husband and dog.

My relationship to cooking is complicated. As a teenager and young adult, I was severely anorexic. I saw myself as disgusting and unworthy of sustenance; at my lowest points I believed sincerely that I should die. Eating one grape more than I had allotted myself could keep me up through the night, wired on pills and pacing, trying to melt away the "extra" calories.

Although my relationship to food has been healthy for over a decade now—going to dinner with my culinarily gifted husband is among my most treasured pastimes—I prefer not to linger too long. The ghost of the person who believed it was right and reasonable to starve herself to death will never fully leave me.

I GREW UP IN A DEEPLY patriarchal family. As a child, I noticed that women were the ones who put in the kitchen time, and it was a miracle if a man ever washed a dish; these structures were simply a given, and for me they chafed.

In college, my then-boyfriend's lament that I did not have home-cooked meals waiting for him when he returned from work was one of many death knells for our relationship. I was trying to get free of something and I didn't know how, and my refusal of the domestic arts felt like the start of a new and possible path. When I left home for graduate school, I stored books in my oven.

At the time, I could not see the other angle—that this refusal also worked to place comfortable limits on my contact with food.

Then a few years ago, I spent a semester at a college in the Hudson Valley, for the most part on my own. A longtime apartment dweller, I had been installed in a house on campus, which meant that for once, I had a real kitchen. One night, I decided to put some vegetables in a pan with olive oil and poke them with a wood spoon and see what happened—the start of a hot meal, it turns out. Some nights a friend and colleague stayed over, and in the mornings it felt good to be able to offer a warm meal to both myself and to someone I cared about. Over the course of the semester, I developed a humble yet sustaining repertoire in the kitchen. Eggs with kale. Eggs with cheese. Eggs with sautéed tomatoes and toast. I was relieved to discover that handling and preparing food was no longer a wellspring of anxiety; it was just, well, food.

TWO WINTERS AGO, I MOVED TO Tennessee for a month to help my mother recover from knee-replacement surgery. My mother, who is in her mid-seventies, spent much of her days lying immobile, hooked up to an ice machine that did little to relieve her pain. She attended agonizing physical therapy sessions almost daily and left each one with a litany of exercises to complete at home. When it was just the two of us, however, she was resistant to doing her exercises. She was resistant to taking her pain medication too, claiming she couldn't stand to feel so foggy. Exhausted from lack of sleep, demoralized by slow progress, my mother was hurting, and it felt slightly treacherous to press her too much on anything.

Her discomfort also found its expression through food. Aware that my culinary skills are lacking, my mother had, before her surgery, amassed a vast amount of frozen casseroles. A week into my tenure, though, the pain dulled her appetite, and all this food was too heavy; she wanted something warm and light.

Perhaps it was my comfort with eggs (at long last I could crack one and see a beautiful yellow-gold yolk and not *seventy-five calories*) that made me think of a frittata, coupled with a vivid memory of a close friend's sister making a frittata the morning she learned their father had suffered a stroke. I had been staying with my friend when she got the call; we went over to her sister's place, and I can still remember the way she moved around the kitchen with a sturdy and capable grace. I can remember her pulling the frittata from the stove and setting the cast iron pan on a hotplate in the center of the table. I can remember adding *learn to offer sustenance to yourself and to others in a time of crisis or really at any time at all* to my "goals for being an actual adult" list.

I spent a morning searching through food sites online and located an appealing—and, crucially, easy-sounding—recipe for a frittata. Spinach and feta and eggs with bell peppers and scallions. Warm and light. For the first time in days, my mother cleaned her plate.

Near the end of my stay, my husband came to visit. By then my mother had improved (and would recover fully, in time). Her physical therapy was less painful; she was able to navigate the house and had even started to walk a little outside, aided by a cane. On the night of my husband's arrival, I picked up ingredients for the frittata and a salad and grabbed a loaf of crusty French bread. My husband watched, incredulous, as I minced vegetables in the kitchen. He asked me if I was feeling well. A little while later, I slid the frittata out of the oven and placed it on the dinner table.

We sat down. I looked around the table and thought, *I love you both so much it hurts.* I thought about my friend's sister. I thought about how sometimes the simple things are the hardest. My husband took a bite and nodded. Later, he even had a second helping. My mom cleaned her plate again. But before all that we raised our glasses and we made a toast to health and we ate.

For My Mother: Spinach and Feta Frittata

1 red bell pepper
1 bunch scallions, sliced
4 tablespoons extra-virgin
    olive oil
1 5-ounce package baby
    spinach

salt and freshly ground
    pepper to taste
8 large eggs
¾ cup water
½ cup feta cheese,
    crumbled

This is inspired by a Food Network recipe. I'm partial to melting extra feta on top. And if you have a magic tip for not slightly burning the bottom, let me know.

Preheat oven to 450°F. Chop the red pepper and scallions. Heat olive oil in a skillet over medium-high heat; add the red pepper, scallions. Stir while they cook for about 4 minutes. Add spinach and sauté for about 2 more minutes, until it wilts. Add salt and pepper to taste and remove from the heat.

Whisk the eggs and water in a large bowl. Add the egg mixture and feta to the skillet and stir to combine. Top with more feta.

Put the skillet in the oven and bake for about 15 minutes, until golden and set.

THE TASTE OF CONSOLATION

CLAIRE MESSUD

Claire Messud's five novels include *The Emperor's Children*, a *New York Times* Book of the Year in 2006; *The Woman Upstairs* (2013); and, most recently, *The Burning Girl* (2017), a finalist for the *Los Angeles Times* Book Award in Fiction. She is also the author of a book of novellas, *The Hunters* (2001). A frequent contributor to *The New York Review of Books* and *The New York Times Book Review*, she teaches creative writing at Harvard University and lives in Cambridge, Massachusetts, with her family.

When I was a child, we moved often on account of my father's work—he was a businessman for a French multinational. For my sister and me, who knew nothing else, this was simply life; but for our mother, who had grown up rooted not just in a city (Toronto) but in a neighborhood (the West End) and more than that, on a block-long crescent (Grenadier Heights) where everyone knew everyone and their business, too—for our mother, this peripatetic existence was a nonsense, and went against her understanding of life altogether.

She was of a generation for which expectations confused, born in 1933 into a culture that required of women chiefly that they marry and bear children; and yet she would see, in her thirties, the lives of women around her radically transformed. My parents' first date, at summer school at Oxford, was a picnic with fellow-student Gloria Steinem and her beau (alas, they did not keep in touch).

My mother's own mother, born more or less with the century, had worked from very early as a secretary, and had, with my grandfather, prolonged their engagement to be sure they had enough money put by so that she could stop working when they married. To be a wife and mother was a privilege and a gift for my grandmother, forced by family circumstances to leave school at sixteen.

Although my mother dreamed of being a lawyer, some part of her must have wanted the trappings of a conventional life—a husband, a couple of children, a dog or two, a nice house. She lived up admirably to the midcentury feminine ideal: a meticulous housekeeper, she ironed even the sheets, our nightclothes, my father's handkerchiefs, the tea towels; she could remove any spot from any fabric; she banished dirt and dust and all foul odors; darned socks and mended moth-holes; she served meals on a military schedule; and she was, indisputably, a fabulous cook. She amassed a collection of over two hundred cookbooks, experimented widely, and as my

French father expected, prepared us three-course suppers every night.

An example: melon with prosciutto, then lamb kidneys in a white wine cream sauce served over rice, with a green salad (a little endive to add texture, and a tarragon vinaigrette, with perhaps a touch of homemade mayonnaise to thicken it); and mixed berries for dessert. Or another: a dressed salad of tiny shrimp and avocado, followed by prune-stuffed pork tenderloin, served with buttered egg noodles and thin-sliced sautéed zucchini topped with parmesan; followed by zabaglione, that airy confection of egg yolks, marsala wine, and sugar, whisked at length over a double boiler, that floats upon the tongue and burns in the throat.

It was my favorite, as a child, and a labor of love, as it could only be made at the last minute. We children would clear the table of the main course; then my mother would disappear to the kitchen for a quarter of an hour. You'd hear the sound of her whisk against the pot, and perhaps the slight banging of the grill on the stovetop as the pot moved. My father would sit at the head of the table and sip his wine; my sister and I would try not to fidget, swinging our legs under the table where our movements could not be seen. When it was time, she'd call us girls to the kitchen to help serve, spooning the bubbling golden froth into small heavy cut-glass bowls that we carried ceremoniously back to the table.

In spite of appearances and her much-praised culinary gift, my mother did not aspire to be a stellar housewife, nor even, particularly, a good cook. Late in life, in the beginnings of the dementia that would take her from us, she marveled at her vast cookbook collection that took up an entire wall in the kitchen: "I don't know why I did it," she said, shaking her head slightly. "I guess it seemed like the thing to do at the time."

When our father traveled on business, my mother took a cooking holiday. She fell eagerly upon the comfort foods of her Canadian childhood, and taught us, by her excitement, that these were the best meals of all: fish and chips wrapped up in greasy newsprint; fat hot dogs tucked in their spongy buns, slathered in ketchup, mustard, and above all relish; shiny onion rings, their slick vegetal innards glistening through the batter; thick milkshakes barely suckable through the straw (chocolate was her favorite, which always seemed rather childish to me); and of course, sweets. Whereas our father preferred cigarettes, and took pleasure only in sophisticated delicacies like chocolate-covered candied ginger or, upon occasion, slivers of the beloved halva of his childhood, our mother loved nothing more than an excellent chocolate brownie, ideally iced.

For a number of years in the early 1970s, from the time I was four until I was nine and a half, we lived in Sydney, Australia. These were our happiest family years, when my parents were still full of hope, and everything seemed still to lie before us. At that time, my mother decided to fulfill her lifelong dream of becoming a lawyer. She enrolled in law school, difficult and demanding on its own, but exponentially more so with two young children and a husband who traveled a great deal for work and had a highly traditional set of expectations for his wife. In those years, my sister and I rode the bus home to an empty house (and made what we called "Russian toffee" for afternoon tea, essentially brown sugar and butter fried in a pan, then cooled in the freezer for as long as our impatience would allow), or upon occasion took a taxi out to the university and waited in the cafeteria for our mother's lectures to end. Having always been punctual, she became the last mother to show up anywhere, and my sister and I were left hanging around at the end of the birthday party, or on the doorstep after the library closed. She still managed to iron the sheets and the nightclothes and whip up the elaborate meals, but certain niceties went by the wayside. She was frequently harried, even grumpy, though never pessimistic. She didn't aim for As, but instead set her sights on Cs: the possible. She compromised and looked ahead.

Then my father was transferred. The story is of course more complicated: in the first Australian years, although my sister and I didn't know it, our mother was particularly bereft (so far from her own mother, in Toronto; and in those days, even the briefest of phone calls was complex and expensive). Before she enrolled in law school, she complained bitterly to my father about having been thus uprooted, dropped on a distant continent with no connections or prospects. He, loving her and trying his best, applied for a transfer, of which no more was heard for a considerable time. Until, of course, it was announced, and intractable. By which point, my mother was just finishing her coursework: only articling for the bar stood between her and her law degree. Suddenly, leaving Australia was a disaster.

> **"The flash of a cardinal in the maple tree; a lone trillium in bloom; a cloud shaped like an old man's head, scudding overhead: These got us through each challenging day."**
>
> – Claire Messud

But leave we did, and moved to Canada, to Toronto, my mother's hometown. There, the university wouldn't accept her Australian coursework (even though both are Commonwealth countries and share a legal system) and told her she would have to begin again. Less hopefully, but doggedly, she rolled up her sleeves and reenrolled. My sister and I, older and more capable, got ourselves to and from school, to and from activities, and entertained ourselves for hours (riding bikes, hitting tennis balls against the garage wall, watching endless reruns of *Get Smart* and *Gilligan's Island*). Our father, meanwhile, inevitably, was within a year transferred again, this time to New York.

What to do? My mother refused to abandon her studies yet again. My father tried to take this in stride—a big step for him, whose own mother had renounced learning to drive so as not to discomfit her husband—and for two years, he commuted weekly to Manhattan: boarding the plane on Sunday night and back again on Friday night, spending the weeks in a bland hotel in midtown,

blocks from his office. My mother became, then, essentially a single parent, although arguably she always had been. Caring for us, she put off her homework till the weekends, when my father, after his lonely week, clamored for her company. They quarreled constantly.

It was in these years that my mother became a devotee of small joys of all kinds and any opportunity for laughter. We sang silly songs in the car, kept our eyes out for eccentric sights in the streets. The flash of a cardinal in the maple tree; a lone trillium in bloom; a cloud shaped like an old man's head, scudding overhead: these got us through each challenging day. But nothing buoyed the spirits—hers or ours—like my mother's chocolate brownies. They were actually Mrs. Hemmings's chocolate brownies, though I never knew Mrs. Hemmings. To this day, the recipe, typewritten on a slip of paper, is glued to the back flyleaf of my mother's battered and stained *Fanny Farmer* (held together with elastic, the masking tape on the spine having long ago failed).

Eventually, my mother dropped

out of law school in Toronto and moved to Connecticut with my father. My sister and I were sent to boarding school. And so she found herself often alone at almost fifty, childless and friendless in a house in the suburbs, her legal studies abandoned and her dreams undone. We were never to mention law school, or the future that might have been. Instead, she set about rebuilding a smaller, private life: always a reader, she volunteered at the local library and got involved in book arts and book design, making local friends with similar interests. She took up photography, became a passionate gardener. She and my father traveled, and she read voraciously the memoirs of nineteenth-century women travelers to faraway places. She wrote many extraordinary letters to her friends, and to us, her daughters, who are lucky now to have them still.

Her chief lesson, though, was "do as I say, not as I do": we understood that she considered her life a failure; and that she greedily wanted, for us, independence and professional success. In her own life, her combination of fatalism and stoicism was powerful, but dark: I adored my mother and we were always close (she was my greatest champion); but I felt for a long time ambivalent about her choices, which seemed to me to lack the very fortitude she so insistently encouraged in us. Now, myself in midlife, so often tired, uneasily attempting to accept life's finitude, I have only compassion and tenderness, and a wistful understanding that external forces often prove greater than ourselves. In her dementia, her utterances often wise, she observed mildly, "There's so much of life to get through, once you realize that your dreams won't come true."

She got through by celebrating the small pleasures: the blooming lilacs; walks with her beloved Jack Russell; a good joke; a good fountain pen; a great literary biography; afternoon tea with Mrs. Hemmings's chocolate brownies. In the end, I've come to feel, life's significance lies chiefly in those small pleasures, and her example is wiser than I once understood.

Mrs. Hemmings's Chocolate Brownies

BROWNIES

1 cup sugar	2 eggs, unbeaten
½ cup cocoa	½ cup chopped walnuts
½ cup flour	pinch salt
½ cup melted butter	1 teaspoon vanilla

Sent to me at boarding school in care packages, these brownies got me through exams, loneliness, even despair. More than a brownie, they're closer to cake, because of the icing, a fudge that melts in the mouth. Nowadays, I only make them occasionally: my children find them too rich, and keen though I am, I can't eat a whole pan myself. But they are unfailingly delicious.

To make them, first sift together: 1 cup of sugar, ½ cup of cocoa, ½ cup of flour. Add butter to dry ingredients. Beat in eggs. Add walnuts, salt, and vanilla. Don't neglect to lightly butter the baking pan. Bake 30 minutes in a 325°F oven.

ICING

3 ounces chocolate	½ teaspoon salt
2 tablespoons butter	1 teaspoon vanilla
2 ½ cups confectioner's sugar	6 tablespoons light cream

For the icing, mix 3 ounces chocolate and 2 tablespoons butter in a double boiler. Combine in blender with 2 ½ cups of confectioner's sugar, ½ teaspoon salt, 1 teaspoon vanilla, and 6 tablespoons light cream. The icing can also be beaten with a Mixmaster, an implement that's easier to clean than a blender.

LONG SLEEVES

MELISSA FEBOS

Melissa Febos is the author of the memoir *Whip Smart* and the essay collection *Abandon Me*, and the recipient of awards from Lambda Literary and the Lower Manhattan Cultural Council. Her work appears in *Tin House, Prairie Schooner, Granta, The Kenyon Review, Lenny Letter, The New York Times, Glamour, Vogue*, and elsewhere. The recipient of fellowships from the MacDowell Colony, VCCA, Vermont Studio Center, Ragdale, the BAU Institute, and others, she is an associate professor at Monmouth University.

One Valentine's Day, I knelt on the bedroom floor of the tiny Brooklyn apartment I shared with my boyfriend, clutching a deboning knife. There was blood under my fingernails. The black trash bag that I'd cut open and laid across the wood floor crinkled under my knees as I stared at twelve pounds of disassembled raw meat in a pool of its own blood. A roll of string, its loose end damp and frayed, lay next to me amid this macabre picnic. On the nearby writing desk my laptop glowed with online instructions for how to debone and tie a pork shoulder.

I had never eaten meat in my life. My mother had raised me vegetarian and I'd never had the urge to break that fast. I didn't find meat particularly gross or offensive; I simply did not identify it as food. I would just as soon have tried to eat pillow stuffing or tree bark. I did not even know that "pork shoulder" existed until the February day that I won it at the local supermarket. The cashier had announced that I was the first customer that day to spend over $100 and could pick out any piece of meat my heart desired. Probably, they had some holiday stock nearing expiration. My first instinct was to decline the prize, but then inspiration struck. I would recoup my winning and cook it for my meat-loving boyfriend. I picked out the largest hunk of dead animal I could find.

"What on earth is that?" my boyfriend asked when I returned home with the boulder of meat.

"Pork shoulder!"

"Yes. But why is it in our apartment?"

"I'm going to cook you a roast for Valentine's Day," I said.

"That's ridiculous."

I shrugged, but did not elaborate. What could I have said? *I am trying to save our relationship by forging one with twelve pounds of dead pig?* It would have been the truth.

Alex and I had met for our first date three years earlier, at a restaurant in the West Village renowned for its vegan fried "chicken." I had chosen the venue

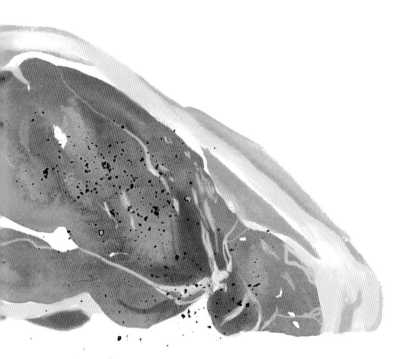

and he, despite being an avid carnivore, had gamely agreed. I was twenty-five years old, in graduate school for creative writing, and had just quit my job as a professional dominatrix, where my shifts consisted of dressing up in corsets, fishnets, stilettos, and the occasional nurse costume to enact the fetishized scenarios of my clients, who were mostly stockbrokers. While it didn't include nudity or technical sex, it was a sex-industry job. Our erotic trade just happened to be golden showers, verbal humiliation, and corporal punishment rather than lap dances or intercourse.

AS WE TRADED BITES OF OUR faux-cutlets, I marveled at how *normal* Alex was. Then I gave him the summary: I had been raised by a Buddhist psychotherapist and a sea captain, dropped out of high school at fifteen to be a writer. I was two years clean and newly returned to the straight working world. Oh, and most of my past lovers had been women.

"Wow," he said. "I never would have thought to drop out of high school to pursue my actual dreams." He had been raised by a banker and a housewife in Westchester and attended the best film program in the country. That is, he had followed his dreams in the manner prescribed by our culture. Though his admiration flattered me, I didn't see my own wayward path as exotic or impressive.

I had always pursued my desires with intense focus, but there is a fine line between confidence and recklessness and I had crossed it a hundred different ways.

I DID NOT HAVE WORDS YET FOR the ways that four years of banking on my body had convinced me that it was my only currency. I had just reentered the *normal* world, and I was prepared to get kicked back out.

Three months after that dinner, we moved into a small one-bedroom in Prospect Heights. The neighborhood, like me, was newly gentrified: in that moment when baby carriages and occasional chalk outlines share the same sidewalks. I could never have afforded the tiny apartment on my adjunct professor salary, but together we could.

The day I first met Alex's parents was warm, midsummer. I stared at my closet that morning, considering the impression I wanted to make. I still had a suitcase of dominatrix outfits under our bed and my arms were covered in tattoos, but I was intent on projecting the woman I was becoming, not the one I was trying to leave behind. I selected a beige silk blouse that buttoned at the wrist and twisted my hair into a chignon.

I have always interviewed well, and that afternoon was no exception. "You don't have to hide your tattoos," Alex said on the train home. "I know," I said. "I just want them to get to know me first. I won't hide them forever."

But a year passed, and then another, and it never seemed like a good time to expand their impression of me. Instead, I accumulated a wardrobe of wrist-length blouses suitable for all kinds of weather.

I also became a cardigan collector. When I started teaching undergraduates, I knew that my personality endeared me to my students; I had passion for my subjects and made them laugh. I knew that I was a good teacher, but still felt marred by my past, afraid that if visible it might invalidate my qualifications. Tattoos don't necessarily boast of a past checkered by spanking men for money or shooting speedballs, but in my mind they did.

Imposter Syndrome: Defined by the American Psychological Association as "an internal experience of intellectual phoniness that appears to be particularly prevalent and intense among a select sample of high achieving women." Unsurprisingly, "societal sex-role stereotyping appear[s] to contribute significantly." Add a history of marketing one's sexuality as primary source of income, and you might understand the fear of blowing my own cover.

The only place where I didn't feel like a double agent was in writing. Instead of tugging down my sleeves, I uncovered things. The page was the only place where I felt free to examine the soft ground between my past and present. I had spent years in different costumes, changing to fit the disparate social landscapes that I inhabited. At my desk, I had no audience but myself.

The first time I wrote about my time as a dominatrix, it poured out of me the way words had in my childhood notebooks. I had never been fully honest with anyone about that experience. I hadn't known how badly I wanted to. When I shared those first pages with a mentor, he said, "You have to write a book. Drop whatever else you are working on."

I didn't want to think about exposing myself so wholly, uncurated by my deep desire to please everyone, to finally pass. I had never been so honest as I was in those pages. When I did think of it, the prospect equally terrified and exhilarated me.

That day a clock started ticking. I knew that such a book would destroy the control I had over how people saw me. There would be no sleeves long enough to draw over those truths.

"It's going to be great," my boyfriend said, not having read a word of it. I nodded. And when I sat at my desk at the foot of our bed and excavated those memories, asked the questions of myself for which I did not yet have answers, it *was* great. But when I stopped writing, I could hear the tick of that clock.

Ten years later, I know that three months is not long enough to know someone. That twenty-five is not old enough to know yourself. But I knew that I loved Alex. He was the first man whom I really trusted. My body had developed early and dramatically as an adolescent and that introduction to the world of male desire—men hollering at me from truck windows when I was twelve, crude gestures in the middle-school hallways—had been a fast and hard lesson in the ways my female body both empowered and disempowered me.

Alex and I made love every night for two of our three years together. In the safety of that love, I discovered my own desire. Not the thrill of making a man who had paid for it crawl across the floor begging. Not the compulsive need to be desired, but desire itself: my own fast breath and hungry hands. I wanted Alex on me, inside me, his hands remaking and holding me in at the same time. I was a feminist. I had been happy to be gay. But though it shamed me, I could not deny the appeal of such simplicity. To be like everyone else.

When I finished the book, he was the first person I showed it to.

"It's great, Melissa," he said. "Though hard to read about those men."

"But I never slept with any of them," I said.

"It's not that. I've just been able to think of that version of you as a different person. My you seemed so separate from those stories."

I wanted to say, *It was a different person!* But I couldn't. For a long time, I had also separated my present self from that past girl. And writing the book had built a bridge between them. To write an honest book, I had had to go back, to look at what that girl had needed, and why she found it in such dark places. I couldn't exile her again.

"I'm really proud of you," he said. Though on the day that the book sold, instead of celebrating, he sank into an inexplicable funk. My excitement fizzled as we ate leftovers in silence. I fell asleep in front of the television, alone.

The next time we sat on his parents' patio eating crudités, I told them that I'd sold a book.

"A memoir," I said. "About my wild college days."

"Oh my," chuckled his mother, an elegant woman with a sleek gray bob. "Well, we will look forward to that."

Over the next few months, Alex and I formulated a plan. There was no hiding the book's subject, but we would give his parents an abridged manuscript—enough material to give them a sense of the storyline while sparing them the details. As we conspired, a part of me wished that I could do the same for my own mother. But she was a therapist who had built her life around hearing the whole truths of other humans. There was no way she would accept a partial truth from me, and ultimately, I was glad for that.

As the publication day neared, I decided to start training for the New York City Marathon. Alex worked longer hours as a video editor. In retrospect, I think we were both afraid that if we stopped moving we would have to face what was happening to us.

This is how a lifelong vegetarian ends up crouched on a garbage bag covered in raw meat on the floor of her own bedroom. I understand why he found it ridiculous—why would I insist on cooking him a meal that I would never myself eat, could not even taste if I succeeded? I couldn't explain why back then, though now it seems obvious: by doing so, I would prove that I could be myself—this weird, queer, kinky combination of things that had no place in the Cheever-esque realm of his upbringing, and still give him what he needed. If I could master those fifteen pounds of meat so outside the realm of my own tastes, maybe I could stay inside a life that didn't quite fit. Of course, it was a doomed effort, but these are the sort of Hail Marys we throw when faced with the hardest dilemmas. It

was me or us, and I didn't want to choose.

The roast came out wonderfully. It was tender and savory and filled our tiny apartment with a delicious and slightly repulsive scent. He barely touched it.

In order to stay in my relationship, I detached from it. I ran and typed and cooked and curled myself against him in sleep. But my heart was already gone. I didn't know that, though, and so when I fell hard in love with a woman who lived down the street, it came as a shock.

Before my book was published, before she and I touched each other, I took him to the house where I was raised, on Cape Cod. Maybe I thought there was a chance that he would see how the past could not be separated from the present. But he didn't. As we sat on a picnic table, ice cream cones dripping down our wrists, I said, "I can't do this."

In the best cases, love leads us to a truer version of ourselves. It seems mercenary to say that the people we love are our teachers, but it is true. They are also whole people, with their own hearts and lessons and breakings. But all I speak for is myself. The way I have gone to the furthest extremes to find my own center.

After I left him, I stopped wearing long sleeves. I stopped offering abridged versions of myself. He had never asked me to do that. But he taught me how to stop.

Slow-Roasted Pork Shoulder

1 pork shoulder
(bone-in, skin-on)

salt and pepper

Preheat oven to 250°F.

Generously season pork shoulder with salt and pepper, then set the pork on wire rack that fits inside a rimmed baking sheet.

Place it in your oven and roast for about 8 hours. (Test readiness by slicing with a knife, or inserting a thermometer—the temperature should read 175°F.)

To get extra-crispy skin once the meat is tender and fully cooked, turn up the oven temperature to 500°F and roast for an additional 15 minutes until the skin crackles. Remove from oven and allow to rest and cool an additional 15 minutes.

Serve.

HOMESICK
AT THE OUTER EDGE
OF THE WORLD

ANTHONY DOERR

Anthony Doerr's most recent book is *All the Light We Cannot See*, which won the 2015 Pulitzer Prize for fiction and was a finalist for the National Book Award. His short stories have appeared in *The Best American Short Stories*, *The O. Henry Prize Stories*, *New American Stories*, and *The Scribner Anthology of Contemporary Fiction*. Doerr lives in Boise, Idaho, with his wife and sons.

For a period of my childhood, somewhere between years eight and nine, and immediately after I read *The Call of the Wild*, I decided I needed to become a mail carrier in the Yukon. I would brave blizzards, pan for gold, never clean my room, and communicate telepathically with my sled dogs. For a week that January I slept with my bedroom window open, to "prepare my body for the cold," until Dad figured out why the house was freezing and put an end to that.

I soon moved on to other dreams—NFL punt returner, myrmecologist, restaurant reviewer who only reviews turkey sandwiches—but the pull of the North never left. Perhaps it was because I grew up in Cleveland, where trekking north on a dogsled would only get me as far as Willoughby, birthplace of Tim Conway, but Alaska loomed mythic in my imagination. It was a place where the sun never set, where auroras sent green curtains as big as cities flapping through the sky, a place as far from the familiar as you could get.

Adolescence compounded things. Nowadays I appreciate Cleveland's leafy, bygone beauty, but as a teenager all I saw were dark Februaries, dead steel mills, and freeways leading elsewhere. I became so enamored with leaving home that I papered my bedroom walls with maps of distant islands and asked my parents questions like, "You mean you were alive at the same time as Jimi Hendrix and you never even tried to see him *once?*"

In the spring of my fourteenth year, I announced that, as soon as summer vacation arrived, I would buy a van with my lawn-mowing earnings and drive to the Arctic Circle. My mother—half-amused, half-horrified—pointed out that I couldn't obtain a driver's license for two more years. Then she stuck a catalog for a summer outdoor leadership school beside my breakfast.

They offered three trips in Alaska. I jabbed my finger at the least scary-looking: a month-long sea kayaking expedition.

Mom said, "You have to be sixteen for that one."

"Oh," I said, and rustled the newspaper classifieds. "Look, here's a minivan for sale. Five hundred bucks."

"Fine," she said, "we'll tell them you're sixteen. But no vans."

Two months later I was standing in the rain wearing two pairs of polypropylene underwear and a life preserver. Ahead of me loomed the bright green fjords of the Tongass National Forest, seventeen million acres, the largest national forest in the United States.

Fifteen of us departed in eleven kayaks and we didn't set foot indoors for a month. Those first days, younger than everybody else, collecting drinking water from creeks and bogs and using rocks and moss as toilet paper, I worried I might have traveled a bit too far from the familiar.

In Cleveland we had beds. We had hot water! We had a vacuum cleaner! What I missed most was food. On our first day, we were divided into three-person tent groups, and each threesome had to pack, protect, and cook its own meals. My tent group was particularly unskilled at food preparation. With our little backpacking stove, we managed to burn every supper: brown rice, lentils, spaghetti, even instant potatoes. Every meal we tried to cook tasted like some variation of burnt noodles. The chocolate we were supposed to ration was gone after the first two nights; we left a two-pound bag of pancake mix uncovered during a rainstorm. I started eating ramen noodles raw, just so they wouldn't take on the burned taste of our pot.

My notebook filled with lists: *Doritos. Pizza. Cheesesteaks.* I had hallucinations about my mother's toffee bars.

By week two, all my tent group had left that remotely resembled dessert were two twelve-ounce bags of just-add-water brownie mix. We "cooked" our first batch by mixing up the batter in our frying pan, putting on the lid, and burying the whole thing in hot embers.

After twenty minutes, the top and bottom were carbonized and the center was raw. Still: ambrosia.

We jammed our second bag of brownie mix into the stern of a kayak where it would be safe from bears and rain, and we pledged not to touch it for another week. Then the weather turned. Stranded in an isolated inlet called Port Malmesbury, on Kuiu Island (population 10), we had rain, and more rain, and high seas. I caught a fever, and couldn't get warm. I was tired of being wet all the time, and hearing the big waves pound the rocks, and not eating potato chips, and the tendrils of homesickness wrapped themselves around my heart.

As dark times go, of course, this was fairly light: our instructors carried a satellite phone in case things got truly dicey; I had two functioning parents who would meet me at the airport when I got home. And among my memories from that month are glories: a humpback whale passing directly beneath my boat, its huge shadow sliding along for what might have been ten full seconds, a galaxy of bubbles rising past the hull. I paddled up a stream so thick with salmon that the blades of my paddle knocked into them. Bald eagles nested above our tent; glaciers gleamed between the high peaks like faraway kingdoms. But when you're fourteen—and shivering, and your sleeping bag is soggy, and your drinking water is brown—relatively non-dire things can feel dire.

Homesickness is an ailment of the stomach as much as of the mind. In the fourth century BCE, with Athenian society in crisis, the ancient Greeks started a new genre of writing, where they imagined fabulous places (often islands) at the outer edges of the world where everyone was happy. Almost all of their utopias featured food. Here's the poet Telecleides, of whose work only a very few fragments remain:

> Every torrent flowed with wine, barley-cakes strove with wheat-loaves for men's lips, beseeching that they be swallowed if men loved the whitest. Fishes would come to the house and bake themselves, then serve

themselves on the tables. A river of broth, whirling hot slices of meat, would flow by the couches; conduits full of piquant sauces for the meat were close at hand for the asking, so that there was plenty for moistening a mouthful and swallowing it tender. On dishes there would be honey-cakes all sprinkled with spices, and roast thrushes served up with milk-cakes were flying into the gullet.

That afternoon at Port Malmesbury, sensing I was sinking, one of my tentmates pulled on her raingear and crawled into her sea kayak and dug out our last bag of brownie mix. The wood was too wet to make a fire, and we were too worn out to light the stove, so we sat in our tent, upended the whole bag into our cookpot, poured in a bit of water, and stirred.

It is no exaggeration to suggest that when I put that first fingerful of raw brownie batter into my mouth, the chemistry of my entire body changed.

Sugar: what humans won't do for it. I think of prehistoric men climbing trees to raid beehives; I think of the "white gold" that drove the transatlantic slave trade. I think of childhood, and what it meant to walk in from a hard day's play to a kitchen full of color and calories, and find my mother making something sweet.

I've heard that a parent's greatest joy in life is watching one's teenagers grow up to have teenagers. My own twin sons are fourteen now and they listen to mumble rap and think Jimi Hendrix was roughly contemporaneous with Mozart, and every day they give me some inkling of what I put my mother through.

When my boys were little, we used to make brownies from a box every couple of weeks. We'd sit on the floor of the kitchen, take out a bowl and spoon, tear open a box of brownie mix, and start stirring. Tonight they sit upstairs playing a video game called Fortnite.

> **"In the spring of my fourteenth year, I announced that, as soon as summer vacation arrived, I would buy a van with my lawn-mowing earnings & drive to the Arctic Circle."**
>
> – Anthony Doerr

Dinner is over; the dishes are done. In a month Henry will leave on a wilderness trip of his own, to Yellowstone, and we won't see him for two weeks.

I preheat the oven. From the pantry I take a box of Duncan Hines Chewy Fudge Family Style Brownie mix and stir it up. Then I walk to the stairs and call up: "I'm making brownies!"

Fortnite sounds drift down the stairs. Gunfire, smack-talk.

"Anybody want to lick the bowl?"

"Um, that's okay, Dad," comes the call back down.

"More for me," I say, though of course the heart fractures a little. The evolutionary reason for adolescence, apparently, is to build a functional, independent adult. It's healthy for teenagers to try to separate from their parents, to critique their clothes, their dance moves, their city.

And so we watch them inch out along the tightrope, doing their damnedest to rebel and conform at the same time.

I sit on the bottom stair and swipe a finger through the brownie batter. As soon as it touches my tongue, time and space collapse. Trees drip, waves crash; I taste that adolescent longing to be elsewhere, pinioned against a craving for the comforts of home.

Brownie Mix

1 box of Duncan Hines Chewy Fudge Family Style Brownie mix

water

Sit on floor.

Cut open bag of brownie mix.

Add water.

Stir.

Eat with fingers.

Repeat when necessary.

A BRIEF RECIPE FOR HAPPINESS

HEATHER SELLERS

Heather Sellers is the author of the memoir *You Don't Look Like Anyone I Know: A True Story of Family, Face Blindness, and Forgiveness*. Her essays appear in *The New York Times*, *The Sun*, *Reader's Digest*, *Redbook*, *Good Housekeeping*, *Tin House*, and *The Best American Essays 2017*. She teaches in the MFA program at the University of South Florida, where she loves to cook with spices.

As a child, I didn't know why my mother locked herself in her closet, or lay looking like a woman made out of wax in her dark bedroom for what seemed like months at a time. When my mother was unwell, I tried to leave her alone, as she wished. I lived on baking chocolate, which I melted in a little copper pan and invested with massive amounts of powdered sugar, and Campbell's cream of celery soups, which I loved.

The bright spot in our home life—the windows were nailed shut, friends were banned from coming inside—was our small galley kitchen. My mother, when she was well enough to come out of the confines of her bedroom, really liked to cook. A deep fryer with oil I never saw changed, not once, sat on the back burner, and in this vessel coated with layers of blackened oil, she made perfect crisp fried chicken with buttermilk, puffy fried mushrooms, crispy French fries. She made custard, homemade applesauce (cinnamon!), and potatoes au gratin. All pale and golden beige, and for a child, all absolutely delicious.

But as I got older, when we went to the grocery store together, I noticed how she furtively inspected every item for signs of tampering. There were many kinds of foods she wouldn't touch and many more she refused to let enter our cart. *That's not coming into my house*, she said, when I held up a tin of oysters, or begged for antipasto salad, ready-made at the deli counter, where my mouth watered.

I yearned to live as girls in novels lived, to go to restaurants, to travel solo, to dine in Europe, drink kir—whatever that was. I wanted to struggle with heartbreak and mountain lions and calico skirts and make vast cauldrons of interesting complexity and eat rabbit and forage for mushrooms and ferns. And I was obsessed with reading cookbooks, planning elaborate meals in my mind. I dreamed of perfecting posole. I wanted to make a Cuban dish I'd read about in a Florida book, with garlic, olives, and pork and plantains over white rice. I begged my mother to let me have a couple of inches of chorizo for experimentation, to let me try fried oysters. She begged me to stop asking her, begged me to stop threatening acts that would despoil her deep fryer forever. *We will never get the smell out of the house.*

Sometimes I got the idea she was hiding from me in the grocery store—I'd see her flicker down the bread aisle, practically racing away. Into her cart I'd sneak wrinkly black jarred olives from Greece, anchovies, tins of sardines. When I found her at the meat counter, ordering a fresh package of ground round (she wouldn't touch the ones that were ready, wrapped, and waiting), I begged her to try *tongue*. I never, not once, got my way.

Where did my adventurous tastes come from? Were they formed in reaction to my mother's strange strictures, a kind of life-giving, rich combination of both nature and creativity? In craving pungent foods few children tolerated, I wonder, was I desperately attempting to make and protect a self that could not just survive, but truly thrive out in the world?

I wanted to be normal *and* I wanted to eat exotic food, which seemed to me to be not a contradiction, but the only solution to my isolated, bizarre upbringing. Happiness in life and exotic foodways were conjoined for me in necessary and mysterious ways. I would eat my way out of my mother's purview, away from her and the bland tyranny of her kitchen, and dine my way into the world. It was as though some part of me knew that to escape her mysterious mental illness, I would be well-served to never eat what she ate. Instead, new things, things that horrified her—these would nourish my spirit and provide my salvation. Buffalo, eel, raw onions, pickled eggs, forbidden grocery-store kimchi—these were the things that attracted me, the flavors that I craved as an elixir, a protective spell.

No, my mother said. That's absolutely not coming into my house.

Under the bare light bulb that lit our shabby yellow kitchen, she buttered her dry toast every morning, and every morning I pulled out leftovers and created one of my breakfast concoctions I called "Kitchen Sink." My mother said

my cooking made her sick to her stomach. Often, she left the room before I'd even settled at the table with my bowl of leftover potatoes, topped with hard-boiled eggs, soy sauce, onions I'd cadged from my hiding place in the pantry.

I was extremely proud of my ability to make something I found sophisticated and interesting from my mother's limited kitchen. But my mother accused me of being like my absent father. He too liked what she called "country cooking," by which my mother meant anything she didn't herself cook: grits, collards, and fish. "Country cooking" also meant things eaten at the times she didn't eat said things—soy sauce at breakfast, poached eggs and bacon for dinner.

Yes, I said. Yes. I *love* country cooking. I *am* country cooking.

By the time I was in junior high school, I was steadfastly practicing what my life would be like when I could move in with my father.

I envisioned parties with canapés, liverwurst and cucumber. I remembered his white plastic sleeve of liverwurst in our fridge

when I was tiny, and pungent cheese, and I longed for him and those flavors, which jolted me into the world. I envisioned him taking me to the Brown Derby, where I'd been once as a tiny child, though I couldn't remember anything except the round bench that formed the seating of the corner booth, and my mother running—actually running—out of the restaurant and not coming back inside; she'd started walking home and we trolled along a busy street, me weeping hysterically in the back, my father insisting she get in the goddamn car, which she did. I didn't yearn to get away from my mother so I could date, go to parties, buy Bruce Springsteen records, dress in tight and low-cut clothes, though I wanted all those things very badly. I wanted to move out of her house and in with my father so I could eat.

When I was fourteen, I found my father, by calling information every day after school and finally getting a number for a Fred Sellers, whom I then called relentlessly. And after endless pleading and haranguing with my mother, fighting, long phone calls from each of us to my father, fits, and so much crying and unhappiness, one afternoon he finally came and picked me up. I had a suitcase and a gigantic stuffed animal, a slender, tall plush cat with green plastic eyes and long eyelashes. I threw Midnight in the back seat and told my father I was starving.

I expected us to go directly to a restaurant—I had several in mind, namely Le Coq au Vin where my French class had gone. My mother hadn't permitted me to go, refused to sign the permission slip. Snails, she said, were known disease carriers; the French did not have our standards of cleanliness or refrigeration.

No, my father said.

At least Red Lobster?

No. For crying out loud, he said. It was the middle of the afternoon. We weren't eating *out.* He acted like I'd asked for a new car. I was shocked and sat in silent shame as we drove across Orlando. But I expected things would turn around when we got to his house, where I envisioned a swimming pool, chaise lounge chairs, ice cubes in tall glasses, well-lit happiness, with endless snacks, chips and cheese, jalapeño peppers, garlic hanging in braids like it did at the Publix deli . . . music playing on the radio.

We pulled up to a row of pink duplexes. A dirt two-track driveway led around to the back. A silver trailer listed to one side behind the far duplex. Trailer parks closed in on either side of the property, and a large jacaranda tree shaded the low-slung buildings. No pool. No lounge chairs. Not even a patio. The highway, which was right across the street, a frontage road, was I-4, and its constant steady traffic sounded like the ocean.

Starving, I followed my father inside, and the torn screen door slammed shut behind us.

"Womp up some dinner," he said, disappearing into his bedroom. I heard the television come on. I stood in the little kitchen, turning in a slow circle. The table was piled high with papers, folders, stacks of mail topped by overflowing plastic ashtrays the size of dinner plates. A pair of jumper cables wandered through the crazy mass of material; no part of the table was visible.

I opened the fridge cautiously. Cartons of milk, orange juice, bottles of beer and tall green bottles of wine, the butt end of a piece of ham, unwrapped. Just sitting there. My mother would die. I knelt before the fridge and inspected every single item. Jars of olives, capers, teeny onions, anchovies, pickles, coleslaw, kimchi, those folded leaves in ruby and green, all packed in together, those strange bright colors from another world. I picked out a jar of herring in sour cream, unscrewed the lid, and right there, on my knees with the fridge door open, I drew out a piece of onion from the milky fishy juice, tilted my head back, and inhaled.

When I went to ask my father what we were doing for dinner, I found him snoring in his bedroom, the bed taking up the entire room.

A fourteen-year-old girl with an ill and distant mother and a passed-out father in a tiny duplex, a new place, can feel both despair and power. I set about to prepare dinner feeling overwhelmed with the chaos and filth and also free, clear, and happy—I was out of my mother's house. In my new kitchen, my first kitchen, I felt I could *reign*. I'd never felt that before. I turned on the radio. Hank Williams, scratchy and too loud. I pulled a bag of flour from the cupboard. Pillsbury Gold Medal All-Purpose flour, the same kind my mother bought. I had no idea what I intended on making—not yet—but flour seemed the logical place to begin my new life, my adult life.

Inside the sealed paper bag, however, I noticed brown-black specks. I cleared some space off the tiny square of countertop by putting the pans and newspapers and magazines on the floor, and I poured some of the flour into a glass and the specks moved about and deep in the flour I could see an entire civilization of bugs with hard bodies, the size of fleas. I screamed and pushed it into the trash.

My father stumbled into the kitchen. He hollered at me for throwing away perfectly good flour and got the bag out of the trash. The bugs, he said, were protein. They'd cook and be fine. The flavor wouldn't be affected—we wouldn't even notice it at all.

I begged him to take us out to eat. Anywhere.

That night, we ate at Moon Palace, and we ate at Moon Palace many nights. Egg foo young and moo shu pork, extra garlic, extra spices, extra heat. He took me to Rossi's for pizza with extra anchovies, extra hot peppers, and to Red Lobster for red snapper.

But my father liked to cook, and in that tiny kitchen, the thing he most liked to cook was a dish he called chicken cordon bleu à la Freddy. He often referred to himself in the third person.

Whenever he deemed the evening a special occasion—my birthday, or his, a day he always called Getting Ready for Freddy Day, or Mark Twain's birthday—or whenever the spirit moved him, he'd get out the glass baking dish and tell me to wash it. As his helper, I knew what came next. I had to find the paper packets of Swiss cheese and ham inside the densely layered wild fridge—pâté, Miller cans, smoked trout, sliced duck, a dozen kinds of mustard, fresh okra, ancient pickled eggs, venison steaks, long past their prime—then carve out space on the countertop and fill a bowl with flour.

I moved very carefully, very watchfully, around flour, around everything in my father's house.

He pounded the chicken breasts on newspaper on the floor.

I sliced and sautéed the mushrooms, careful to make sure each one was the same width, had the same amount of real estate around it in the bubbling butter.

He draped each chicken breast with first a slice of ham and then a slice of cheese. I rolled the meat and tooth-picked the parcels tightly shut with four toothpicks per breast. He poured the wine over the bundles, holding the bottle high, dramatically polishing off the rest of the contents, drinking straight from the bottle, laughing, spilling, dancing his way over to the oven with the feast, and then he poked the pan into the heat.

I cleared off the table, or rather carved out space in the piles for our plates and silverware. I boiled the noodles and made salads and he talked and talked and talked and drank gin and talked.

When it was time, he pulled the hot pan from the oven. He poured the sauce over the breasts on their beds of noodles and poked his fingers into the gravy boat and licked them and swooned. *Now girl chile, this is some good eatin'!*

In that tiny, jam-packed apartment, alone with my father, eating off dinner plates that came from a grocery store promotion (twelve cents apiece), under a buzzing fluorescent light, the traffic a constant low storm outside, we sat down before the plates of chicken cordon bleu, rich and glistening with the wonderful sauce, and I knew. I knew I had a map for my life on those plates and that if we could manage this, I could make a life. I would simply make more, and more, and more of this, just this. Slowly, I'd keep pushing the chaos back, making more room on the table.

Chicken Cordon Bleu

Preheat oven to 350°F.

Gather:

chicken breasts	sliced ham
flour	sliced Swiss cheese
olive oil	white wine
diced white onion	egg noodles
butter	parsley
fresh button mushrooms	

Take chicken breasts (one or two for each person) and pound them flat. Dredge in flour and sauté in olive oil, turning after lightly browned. The onions can cook in this same pan.

In another sauté pan, melt the butter on low heat and sauté sliced mushrooms—don't crowd the pan; don't let them touch each other.

Lay a slice of ham and then a slice of cheese on each flat breast; fold in half and secure with toothpicks. Set in a greased baking dish. Deposit the mushrooms and pan drippings from both pans over the breasts all nestled in the baking dish. Pour white wine and a little olive oil over all of that.

Bake for 30 to 45 minutes while you boil the egg noodles. Add a little butter and fresh finely chopped parsley to the noodles and serve the breasts on beds of noodles, with the sauce on the side in a gravy boat.

MEALS OF MY TWENTIES

CARMEN MARIA MACHADO

Carmen Maria Machado's debut short story collection, *Her Body and Other Parties*, was a finalist for the National Book Award and the winner of the National Book Critics Circle's John Leonard Prize. Her essays, fiction, and criticism have appeared in *The New Yorker*, *The New York Times*, *Granta*, *Tin House*, *The Believer*, *Guernica*, and elsewhere. She is the Writer in Residence at the University of Pennsylvania and lives in Philadelphia with her wife.

My friend Sarah and I moved to California when I was twenty-one. We'd both come directly from college, deciding to try living as far from our previous city—Washington, D.C.—as we possibly could. D.C. was muggy and conservative and full of mosquitoes and politicians, and our little apartment on the Oakland/Berkeley border was free of all of those things. We grew basil in the alley behind the kitchen, and then we killed some flowers and succulents and eventually the basil, too.

Sarah taught me to make alfredo from scratch, running crushed garlic through a slick of butter and sprinkling flour into the pan. The smell of it—the warmth of the garlic, the slow, browning burble of the butter—was practically tangible; it felt like it could lift me up from the ground like the scent of pie cooling on a windowsill in an old-timey cartoon. I had never seen anyone make alfredo from scratch. In fact, I don't think I realized alfredo *could* be made from scratch, that it didn't spontaneously manifest in jars in the supermarket.

She made other things, too: tortellini soup, beautiful salads, stir-fry, all of which she shared with me. She shared everything; she was so lovely and kind and generous it made my teeth hurt. I think I loved her, a little. I tried to repay her in kind, but then nearly destroyed the kitchen making frozen pot stickers—I dropped water into the hot oil and a column of flame erupted from the pan. I didn't burn down the apartment, but only just. The pot stickers were scorched, but edible. Afterward, I had to Google my mistake, which I truly did not understand.

Half a year into this new life, I met a chef who was struggling financially and moving back in with his parents in the Midwest. He invited me to his apartment. He was tall and sad and sweet and showed me what he was giving away with his hands shoved deep into his pockets. I took most of it: giant pickle jars filled with endless varieties of bougie and exotic flours; herbs and spices; huge stock pots; a set of knives. I was astonished at the size of my windfall. I tried to offer him money. "I'm just happy someone will use it," he said, looking every bit the part of a forlorn fairy godmother.

My boyfriend and I cooked together, but when I probe my memory for what we made I can't conjure up anything, as if our breakup—and there was a breakup, a terrible and humiliating first heartbreak that I was sure would kill me dead—wiped the meals away. Dear friends came to my house, helped me clean up, dribbled drops of Rescue Remedy into tall glasses of water, fed me because I couldn't remember how to feed myself. Mourning, I bought Black Phoenix Alchemy Labs samples, called imps, and spent my days watching *Buffy the Vampire Slayer* and reviewing the perfumes on my LiveJournal and barely eating anything at all.

When I returned to my body, I threw my energy into cooking. The dear friends who'd helped me pick up my life cooked for me in their sunny San Francisco condo, and I imitated their meals until I began to learn. I looked up recipes on the internet. I practiced. It helped that I was a thirty-second walk from the legendary Berkeley Bowl, whose heaps of produce and plenty remains the only thing I miss about the Bay Area. I fed myself like a woman who needed to love the world again. I made fresh lo mein tossed with sautéed broccolini, soy sauce, ginger, sriracha; corn tortillas warmed in a pan and loaded with warmed and spiced refried beans, chunks of creamy avocado, twists of lime; elaborate salads with golden beets and goat cheese and walnuts, tossed with goddess dressing and robust,

> "The egg arranged so the hot yolk would ooze & you could drag the sandwich through itself like a medieval torture technique."
>
> – Carmen Maria Machado

garlicky croutons. I bought produce I didn't know how to cook or eat. Googled it. Found new obsessions, spit others into the sink. Smelled the durian with longing—the scent incredible to me, overly sweet and meaty—but never could afford to buy one. I bought salad mixes with edible flowers from the farmers market and stood over the counter in my cottage's kitchen, nibbling at the petals like I imagined a snail would. The meals were overwhelmingly vegetarian—my ex-boyfriend was a vegetarian, the son of Seventh-day Adventists, and I'd gotten used to it. I learned to like wine. At least, I learned to like two-dollar bottles from Trader Joe's, which was all I could afford.

But I wanted to get out of California. I hated my job, I hated the Bay Area, I hated my life. I visited a grad school in Texas and came back making the sandwich my host had made for me: an over-easy egg on toasted English muffin with a smear of mustard and mayonnaise, topped in melted sharp cheddar cheese, the egg arranged so the hot yolk would ooze and you could drag the sandwich through itself like a medieval torture technique.

I didn't choose that grad school, though. I went to Iowa instead. There, my roommate John and I made ridiculous foods. He fermented his own sauerkraut and made jam-and-grilled-cheese sandwiches using Eggo waffles as the bread. We made soups and chicken dishes and pasta and embraced the smorgasbord, hunched over a table of miscellaneous pleasures like urchin children. At the edge of town, I went to people's houses and snipped green beans from their vines and once filled an entire garbage bag with unwanted basil and made a massive supply of pesto that lasted the whole winter. I briefly lived with a woman who made me miserable but introduced to me to tomato-eggplant pasta with pine nuts and Mediterranean-style

couscous and roasted guinea hen and a feta peppercorn dip that gave me tremendous farts.

I closed out the decade with my now-wife, Val. She loves to cook with me and for me and I for and with her. She is excellent at turning random scraps of leftovers into something interesting. "This is a Val dish," she'll say, and it always means, *This could be anything, but I think it's going to be pretty good; also, the kitchen is now a disaster.* I prefer the order of recipes, the serene logic of them. I try to clean as I go. That's just how it is. We're not in our twenties anymore.

IN *THE FIFTH ELEPHANT*, TERRY Pratchett quipped: "He'd noticed that sex bore some resemblance to cookery: it fascinated people, they sometimes bought books full of complicated recipes and interesting pictures, and sometimes when they were really hungry they created vast banquets in their imagination—but at the end of the day they'd settle quite happily for egg and chips, if it was well done and maybe had a slice of tomato."

I have always loved a box of Kraft Macaroni & Cheese. It was something my mother kept on hand in case she was too tired to cook, or if she needed us to feed each other. It was the first thing I learned how to make on my own; at least, the first thing that had ingredients and steps, and didn't just need to be heated up. I have never stopped making it; even in between my increasingly sophisticated culinary experiments, I always have one or two boxes in the cupboard, for emergencies of the body and spirit.

In this recipe, the addition of tomato soup, garlic powder, and black pepper gets the dish closer to another comfort food of mine: SpaghettiOs. It is creamy and cheesy and acidic and peppery. Tense peas give you tiny bursts of sweetness, and the frozen ones are just as good as fresh for this purpose; sliced-up hot dogs give you chunks of salt, though of course vegetarians can forgo the hot dogs. (I have never liked tofu dogs and I don't recommend them. I always thought that hot dogs would be the easiest meat to reproduce for herbivores—after all, they bear zero resemblance to the creature of their origins—but I have yet to find a decent substitute with that same pleasant, rubbery give and salty body.) You can substitute the frozen peas with frozen corn in a pinch, but it's not as good.

This is a thing I make for myself when I'm sad or sick or I've had a terrible day. It's also endlessly adaptable and can technically all be made in a single pan if you want to minimize cleanup. I hope it brings you some measure of nostalgia and comfort.

You-Are-Ten-and-Tender-and-Can-Only-Make-This-One-Thing and Cheese

box of Kraft Macaroni &
   Cheese, or equivalent
   (I prefer the pasta
   shapes in this order:
   shells, special-edition
   shapes, spirals; the
   macaroni version is
   by far the worst and
   should be avoided at
   all costs)

tomato soup
butter
black pepper
garlic powder
hot dogs (optional)
peas (optional)

Prepare the macaroni and cheese as you would normally: boil the water, add the pasta. Separately, heat a small saucepan with a small amount of tomato soup. (If you are adding hot dogs and peas, you can cook them with the pasta or with the soup.) When the noodles are tender, drain the water, and then whisk butter in the mess of them until melted. Add the powdered cheese. Instead of adding milk to dissolve the powder, add the tomato soup to desired taste and texture—I like mine slightly soupy. If you add hot dogs, slice them into little rounds before stirring them in. Add freshly cracked black pepper and garlic powder to taste. Don't add salt—it's got plenty of salt already. Serve in a bowl; eat hot. Think about your past self with compassion. She got you here, after all.

Loss

DESSERT

COLUM McCANN

Colum McCann is the author of six novels, three collections of stories, and one book of advice for budding writers. Born and raised in Dublin, Ireland, he has been the recipient of many international honors, including the National Book Award, the International Dublin Impac Prize, a Chevalier des Arts et Lettres from the French government, election to Aosdana, the Irish Arts Academy, several European awards, the 2010 Best Foreign Novel Award in China, and an Oscar nomination. In 2017 he was elected to the American Academy of Arts. His work has been published in over forty languages. He is the cofounder of the nonprofit global story exchange organization Narrative 4, and he teaches at the MFA program in Hunter College.

The sky would always be this shade of blue. The towers had come down the day before. Third Avenue on the Upper East Side was a flutter of missing faces, the posters taped to the mailboxes, plastered on windows, flapping against the light poles: "Looking for Derek Sword"; "Have You Seen This Person?"; "Matt Heard: Worked for Morgan Stanley." The streets were quieter than usual. The ash fell, as ash will.

Everything felt honed down to the necessary, except for one woman who sat alone at an outdoor table in a restaurant on Seventy-Fourth Street. She had just ordered a piece of chocolate cake. It arrived in front of her, and the waiter spun away. A slice of two-layer cake. Dark chocolate. A nipple of cream dolloped on top. A sprinkling of dark powder.

The woman was elegant, fiftyish, beautiful. She touched the edge of the plate, brought it toward her.

At any other time, it would have been just a piece of cake, a collision of cocoa and flour and eggs. But so much of what the city was about had just been leveled—not just the towers but a sense of the city itself, the desire, the greed, the appetite, the unrelenting pursuit of the present. The woman unrolled a fork from a paper napkin, held it at her mouth, tapping the tines against her teeth. She ran the fork, then, through the powder, addressing the cake, scribbling her intent.

Our job is to be epic and tiny, both. The ordinary shoves up against the monumental. Three thousand lives in New York had just disintegrated into the air. Nobody could have known it for certain then, but hundreds of thousands of lives would hang in the balance—in Baghdad, Kabul, London, Madrid, Basra. When big things fall, they shatter into fragments. They crash down and scatter over a very large landscape. It was apparent, even one day after the attacks, that so much of the world had felt the impact.

Still, there is a need, now and always, for sharply felt local intimacies. I stood by the corner and watched the woman's dilemma. It could have been grief, it could have been grace, or even a dark, perverse sense of humor. She held the forkful of cake for a very long time. As if it were waiting to speak to her, to tell her what to do. Finally, she ate a bite of it. She sat looking into the distance. She pulled her lips along the silver tines to catch whatever chocolate remained there, then turned the fork upside down, ran her tongue along it. It was the gesture of someone whose body was in one place, her mind in another. She pierced the cake again.

The darkness rose over the Upper East Side. The woman finished her dessert. She didn't pinch the crumbs. She placed the fork across the plate. She paid. She left. She didn't look at anyone as she turned the corner toward Lexington Avenue, but she still returns to me after all this time, one corner after another, almost two decades now.

My mind is decorated with splinters. Another long series of wars, another short distance traveled. We do not necessarily need anniversaries when there are things we cannot forget. Yet I also recall this simple, sensual moment. I still have no idea—after almost two decades of wondering—whether I am furious at the woman and the way she ate chocolate cake, or whether it was one of the most audacious acts of grief I've ever seen.

Chocolate Cake

⅔ cup butter, softened

1 ⅔ cups white sugar

3 large eggs

1 teaspoon pure vanilla
 extract

2 cups all-purpose flour

⅔ cup cocoa powder

1 ¼ teaspoons baking
 soda

1 teaspoon sea salt

1 ⅓ cups milk

your favorite chocolate
 frosting

Preheat your oven to 350°F and grease and flour a 13-by-9-inch pan; set aside.

In a mixing bowl, combine the butter and sugar. Mix thoroughly. Then add the eggs one at a time along with the vanilla extract, beating well.

In another bowl, combine the flour, cocoa powder, baking soda, and salt, and add this to the creamed mixture. Add the milk last and beat until smooth. Pour the batter into your prepared pan.

Bake at 350°F until a toothpick comes out clean, approximately 35–40 minutes. Then remove from the oven and allow it to cool for 10 minutes in the pan before inverting onto a wire rack to cool completely.

Top with your favorite chocolate frosting: perhaps one that is slightly bitter.

GENERAL TSO

LEV GROSSMAN

Lev Grossman is the author of five novels, including the international bestseller *Codex* and the number one *New York Times* bestselling Magicians trilogy. The Magicians books have been published in twenty-five countries, and a Syfy series based on the trilogy premiered in early 2016. A widely published journalist, Grossman spent fifteen years as the book critic and lead technology writer for *Time* magazine. Born and raised in Lexington, Massachusetts, he lives in Brooklyn with his wife, two daughters, and one son.

When you get divorced, if you don't get the house or the apartment, what you get is a divorce apartment. Generally speaking it's a relatively small and crap apartment, reflecting your newly remade financial situation. In fact your divorce apartment will probably resemble the kind of apartment you lived in during your twenties, except that it now contains a you who is no longer in your twenties.

You may or may not deserve all this.

An architect-designed restaurant-style kitchen was not a feature of my divorce apartment. In my old life I liked to cook most of my meals, but after I got divorced I ordered takeout most nights. On two out of three of those nights what I ordered was General Tso's tofu.

Why General Tso's tofu? Partly because it was there: they had it at the veggie storefront Chinese joint a few doors down, which for some reason had a life-size plaster Egyptian sarcophagus outside it, and which was staffed by young, beautiful, unsmiling Chinese women who spoke no English.

Partly because it had tofu in it, so I could tell myself it was basically healthy. (It wasn't. It's possible, with strenuous effort and painful compromises, to make a low-calorie, low-sodium General Tso's tofu, but this wasn't that.)

But mostly I ordered it because I loved it and it made me feel good. It was easy to get depressed in the divorce apartment. I was alone. I missed my daughter. I was mourning a complicated eleven-year series of major personal mistakes. I was newly poor and my apartment sucked. And General Tso's tofu, when made properly, is stunningly delicious.

There isn't much that's authentically Chinese about General Tso's tofu. There was a real General Tso, who had a very successful career suppressing a lot of internal revolts in China and died in 1885. (According to Wikipedia he had a long and happy marriage. Good for him.) But he never tasted the tofu that bears his name. General Tso's chicken was invented in New York in the 1970s and the tofu version came sometime after that. It doesn't exist in China.

But this inauthenticity withers into irrelevance in the face of General Tso's greatness as a dish.

The essence of General Tso's Anything is the sauce: sweet, sour, spicy, salty, unabashedly gluey, studded with nuclear red chilies. Its color is a radiant translucent orange that reminds one of rubies and molten iron. The hot tofu, lightly coated in a form-fitting cornstarch batter, cracks open to reveal a silky slippery interior not unlike a savory toasted marshmallow. Interleave it with some hastily blanched broccoli to add texture and vegetal credibility and you have a perfect one-dish meal.

To me in my divorce apartment General Tso's tofu was like an edible antidepressant. I could eat any amount of it, hunched over a trestle table, watching nihilistic British sitcoms on YouTube, using Wi-Fi borrowed from my neighbors.

The divorce apartment is not a permanent thing. Eventually your finances will stabilize and you'll realize you could probably afford something slightly better, or you'll move in with somebody who can. I can't remember the last time I ate General Tso's tofu in my divorce apartment, but the night before I moved out I was on my way to dinner with my then-girlfriend, now-second-and-final-wife, when I passed the Chinese restaurant with the Egyptian sarcophagus in front.

Someone hailed me: it was one of the women who worked behind the counter.

"Hey!" She was smiling. "Aren't you coming? We make it for you already! General Tso!"

I was so surprised that she could speak English that I temporarily forgot how to speak English myself. I just smiled and waved and made some gesture along the lines of: *What can you do, these things happen, I couldn't stay depressed and divorced forever, eventually I had to eat some non-comfort food. But I'm really grateful for all the comfort food you made me.*

I hope she understood.

General Tso's Tofu

It took me at least a dozen tries to recreate proper Chinese-restaurant General Tso's tofu at home without resorting to lethal levels of sugar and oil and cornstarch. Look online and you'll see a million different recipes with stuff like ketchup and pineapple and tamarind in them.

You don't need any of that stuff. As it turns out, making a great General Tso isn't actually all that hard. The recipe below leans heavily on the version of General Tso's chicken that was worked out by the great J. Kenji López-Alt, whose large white cookbook *The Food Lab* I recommend very highly.

First, make the sauce. You'll need:

3 tablespoons soy sauce
2 tablespoons cooking
    sherry
2 tablespoons rice vinegar

3 tablespoons chicken stock
    (you can use the bought
    stuff)
4 tablespoons sugar
1 teaspoon roasted sesame oil
1 tablespoon cornstarch

Throw all that stuff in a bowl. Stir it till the sugar and cornstarch dissolves. Set it aside. Its moment is coming.

Next, take:

2 cloves of garlic
a chunk of fresh ginger,
    maybe an inch long
a bunch of scallions

a handful of dried red chilies
    (Like a real handful. More
    than you would think. López-
    Alt recommends eight, and
    I think that's a minimum.
    You don't necessarily eat
    the things, but they create
    the ambient heat that's so
    essential to this dish. Also
    they look cool.)

Mince the garlic. Mince or grate the ginger. Chop the scallions into one-inch chunks. (You can mince some of them too and save them for garnish if you're fancy.) Throw garlic, ginger, scallions, and chilies into a frying pan. Sweat them in a little vegetable oil for a minute or two.

Then pour in the sauce. Let the whole thing become warm and awesome together, which will take about a minute, then turn off the heat.

Then—or you can do this at the same time—cook the tofu.

The part of any General Tso's tofu recipe that requires serious patience and chops is giving the tofu a light crispy coating. But guess what? *I don't bother!* Is it less authentic that way? *Yes it is.* But here's the thing: to get that coating you have to fry it, and I don't fry shit. I just don't.

It's not worth it. Plus I mean, Jesus, when you're divorced you gotta cook healthy. You gotta get back in the game. You're not gonna fry your way back there.

So anyway take the tofu, a pound of it. Press it under a heavy plate or something for maybe 10 minutes to squeeze out extra moisture. While this is happening put some water on to boil and cut up a head of broccoli into florets. You're gonna want to blanch them for 4 minutes at some point along the way.

Once the tofu has been squeezed, cut it into ¾-inch cubes. Throw the cubes into a bowl, toss them with a little cornstarch, then throw them in a nonstick pan with a bit of vegetable oil. Cook on medium-high heat for 4 or 5 minutes, till the tofu is just starting to color on one side.

(Every recipe anywhere will tell you to use firm tofu for this. Literally every one. You can. It's easier and it won't break up in the pan. Personally I use silken tofu—I love its soft frictionless gloss, and the way it integrates with the sauce. If you use it, I warn you, it will not stay in neat cubes, it will fall apart. It'll be messy. It won't look as nice. I use it anyway.)

Once the tofu is cooked, put it into the sauce. Throw the broccoli—that broccoli you blanched for 4 minutes—in after it. Integrate. You're done! It snuck up on you, didn't it.

Serve it in a bowl. A nice bowl—come on, you've still got your pride. Place it on the table, maybe with some white rice. Place a beer next to it. Now you're really done.

Tuck in. Whoever you are, whatever you have or haven't done, whatever your apartment looks like, you made this, and you deserve to enjoy it. Don't despair. There are better times ahead.

FRIENDS, GRIEF, AND GREEN CHILIES

ROSIE SCHAAP

Rosie Schaap is the author of the memoir *Drinking with Men*, named one of the best books of 2013 by *Library Journal* and National Public Radio. She was the "Drink" columnist for *The New York Times Magazine* from 2011 to 2017, and her byline has also appeared in *Food & Wine*, *Lucky Peach*, *Saveur*, and *Travel + Leisure*, among other publications. Schaap is on the faculty of the MFA program in creative writing at Fairleigh Dickinson University.

Early in 2010, newly widowed and drowning in the thick fog of grief, I had what I now recall as one quick, crisp moment of clarity and calm. Setting aside the piles of bills and condolences mounting on my kitchen table, I emailed a dear old friend and asked if I might come to stay with her and her family for a week in Santa Fe the following month. The desert seemed as far away as I could get from home, which no longer felt quite like home, but had become the seat of my sadness, the dwelling place of my mourning. Teri, my friend in New Mexico, didn't hesitate before saying yes. I booked my flight and sank back into despondency.

But as the day of the trip grew closer, I realized that I hadn't been quite as clearheaded as I thought when I planned the trip: it turned out I'd be in Santa Fe during Passover, and I didn't want to forgo the holiday. I emailed Teri again, and asked if we could have a seder at her house. Again, she said yes—an enthusiastic yes: She'd never been to a seder. Teri is Native American, a member of the Kiowa tribe; her husband, Dennis, is Odawa-Ojibwe. They were raising their two young sons to know and honor their native heritage. Teri said she'd invite her mother, too.

So now I was headed to the desert not only to get away. I was also going to spend Passover there. It's a tradition of the holiday—if not a prerequisite—to welcome strangers to the seder, and that can mean many things, but often it means inviting non-Jews to the table, too. In Santa Fe, the proportions would be reversed: I would be the only Jew at the table, celebrating with a Native American family.

By then, Passover mattered to me. That was not always so. I'd grown up in a pretty secular New York City Jewish household. We celebrated Passover, but never made a big fuss about it. When I was a kid, we usually wound up at the home of older relatives, and, in truth, I mostly remember being bored, at least until the time came to hunt for the afikomen (a half of a matzo hidden away early in the seder, which the children are asked to find afterward, and for which they are given small gifts in reward—like candy or change). But at a certain great-aunt and great-uncle's apartment, even that didn't hold out much excitement: I was well aware, year after year, that the afikomen was nestled inside the piano bench, wrapped in a napkin, tucked into some sheet music.

My feelings about Passover grew fonder in college, where one of my dormitory mates presided over a casually exuberant seder in our dorm living room each year. There wasn't a full feast, and weed played the role of bitter herbs, but we read selections from the Haggadah (the seder text, which includes a telling of the story of the Jews' liberation from slavery in Egypt), and sang traditional Passover songs, and drank kosher wine with gusto. It may have been untraditional, but it connected me more deeply both to the holiday's immense capacity for joyfulness and—even in its loose, playful way—to its significance as a celebration of freedom.

When I moved back to New York after college, I found myself at seders that fulfilled the promise of those dorm Passovers, minus the marijuana: similar in spirit and openness and inclusiveness, but accompanied by tremendous, delicious feasts of matzo ball soup and brisket and charoset (the sweet blend of fruits and nuts and honey and wine, meant to represent the mortar used by the Jews during their slavery) and macaroons. At these seders, we read the Haggadah in its entirety, and I found the stories and the rituals riveting.

I arrived in Santa Fe with a seder plate and a Haggadah. Seeing my old friend waiting for me outside her cozy home in the hills just outside the city had exactly the effect I'd hoped for. I felt a great rush of gratitude: for her friendship and hospitality; for the high, clear air; for the vital and soothing distance from home, from the everyday difficulty of mourning, from the now-uneasy familiarity of life in New York.

Teri had already explained to her sons—Ahbedoh, nine, and Nimkees, seven—what they might expect at the seder, and they seemed excited about it, too. I woke up early on the morning of the second day of Passover and got to work on our dinner right away. First, I made the chicken stock for the matzo ball soup (Teri raises chickens, so it was the best and freshest I'd ever made). Next, the charoset, a Sephardic-inspired variation with apricots and pistachios, saffron and mint.

> "A widow is always a kind of stranger: perceived as set apart, different, to be pitied. I had started to see myself that way, too."
>
> – Rosie Schaap

And while the stock simmered, I started on the dinner's star: a massive beef brisket that would cook slowly over low heat for many hours, with an abundance of onions I'd already cooked down so they had caramelized slightly, carrots and beef stock and bay leaves. But since I was in New Mexico, where the local green chilies are so wonderful, shouldn't I spice it up a little? I chopped up some green chili and added it to the pot.

Many hours later, we all sat down for the seder. We took turns reading from the Haggadah. Teri's mother, a gifted storyteller, read about the ten plagues with dramatic flair. And the two little boys at the table patiently took in the whole story of exile and liberation, of life and death, its meaning not lost on them.

To me, the most stunning moment among many in the Haggadah is this: This is the bread of affliction eaten by our ancestors in the land of Egypt. Whoever is hungry, let him come and eat.

Whoever is needy, let him come and join in the observance of Passover.

My own affliction could not compare to that of my exiled ancestors, but as I ate matzo that night, I considered that I had arrived in New Mexico feeling wounded and heartsick. A widow is always a kind of stranger: perceived as set apart, different, to be pitied. I had started to see myself that way, too. But here in New Mexico, I felt none of that; instead, I felt only comfort and compassion.

I can't say that the seder vanquished my grief, but, for one night spent eating delicious food with caring friends, who had so openheartedly indulged me in this ancient ritual of my ancestors, I felt freed from despair. The next day, when I saw nine-year-old Ahbedoh walking to school with charoset and matzo tucked into his backpack for his afternoon snack, I even felt joyful again. And ever since my Santa Fe seder, I've never made a Passover brisket without green chili.

Santa Fe Seder Brisket

1 4- to 5-pound beef
    brisket
kosher salt
freshly ground black pepper
4 tablespoons vegetable oil
2 large onions, coarsely
    chopped
2 cloves garlic, minced

2 to 3 New Mexico green
    chilies, seeded and
    minced
2 medium carrots, peeled
    and coarsely chopped
3 tablespoons tomato paste
3 cups beef stock
2 bay leaves

Preheat oven to 325°F.

Season the brisket liberally with salt and pepper.

On the top of the stove, warm a large Dutch oven (one that has a lid) over medium-high heat. Add 2 tablespoons of the oil; when it shimmers a bit, add the brisket and brown it, about 5 minutes on each side. Turn off the stove. Remove brisket to a platter.

Wipe out the Dutch oven with paper towels and return to stove. Over medium heat, add the remaining oil, the onions, and a few pinches of salt and pepper. Cook onions until they are soft and translucent, about 20 minutes. (Keep an eye on them and stir occasionally; don't let them burn. Lower heat if necessary.)

Add garlic, chilies, carrots, and tomato paste; give it all a stir. Return the brisket to the Dutch oven; add the beef stock and the bay leaves. (If there's not enough stock to cover the beef, add water until it's covered by about half an inch.)

Cover the Dutch oven, and put it in the oven. Turn the meat every half hour or so, and cook until it's tender enough to pull apart with a fork, about three and a half hours.

Remove the brisket to a platter to let it rest. Over high heat, cook the gravy down until it thickens, about 10 minutes, stirring occasionally and scraping any bits at the bottom of the pan. Taste the gravy, and add salt and pepper as necessary. Remove and discard the bay leaves. (Optional: I like to purée the gravy with an immersion blender, but if you prefer a chunkier gravy, it's fine to leave it as is.)

Slice the meat, return it to the gravy, and serve.

SIERRA LEONE, 1997

CHIMAMANDA NGOZI ADICHIE

Chimamanda Ngozi Adichie has published three novels: *Purple Hibiscus*, *Half of a Yellow Sun*, and *Americanah*, which won the National Book Critics Circle Award and is being made into a film. Ms. Adichie is also the author of the story collection *The Thing Around Your Neck*. Adichie's 2012 TED Talk "We Should All Be Feminists" started a worldwide conversation about feminism and was published as a book in 2014. Her most recent book, *Dear Ijeawele, or a Feminist Manifesto in Fifteen Suggestions*, was published in 2017. A recipient of a MacArthur Foundation Fellowship, Adichie divides her time between the United States and Nigeria.

It was a Saturday in 1984. I was playing with my little brother, Kenechukwu, near the water tank in our large, flower-filled compound in Nsukka—the dusty, serene university town in eastern Nigeria where I grew up. My mother stood by the back door and said, "*Bianu kene mmadu.*" Come and greet somebody. Our new houseboy had arrived. He was sitting on a sofa in the living room, his legs cradling a black plastic bag that held his belongings.

"Good afternoon," Kenechukwu and I said. "*Nno.*" Welcome.

Later, after my mother showed Fide his room, in the detached boys' quarters behind the house, she told us, "Fide has come from the village and he has never seen a telephone or a gas cooker. So we will all help teach him and get him settled."

I stared at Fide, fascinated. Our former houseboy, who had left the week before after stealing some money from my father's study, had been knowingly urban; he had sometimes even fixed the stereo. Fide had never seen a refrigerator. He was light-skinned, and his lips were so thick and wide they took up most of his face. He spoke a rural dialect of Igbo that was not Anglicized, like ours, and he chewed rice with his mouth open— you could see the rice, soggy like old cereal, until he swallowed. When he answered the phone, he said, "Hold on," as we had taught him to, but then he dropped the receiver back on the cradle. He washed our clothes in metal basins, and pegged them on the line tied from the mango to the guava tree in the backyard. It took him hours. At first, my mother shouted, "Don't stop your work to stare at every single lizard that goes by!" Later, she left him alone until he was done.

Kenechukwu and I sat on the steps while he worked. On hot afternoons when the sun made topaz patterns on the glass louvers of the kitchen, Fide told us stories about birds—folk stories in which birds flew up to the sky to ask God for rain, and nature stories in which birds made their nests

with bits of hair they had picked up outside the barber's hut in his village. "I can catch some birds for you," he said. And he dropped bread crumbs in a staggered line from the dustbin outside, up the short steps that led to the house, through the open back door, and into the kitchen. He crouched behind the door. When the birds arrived in the kitchen, he slammed the door and dashed after them. Once, he cracked a louver; once, he tore the mosquito netting on the window; once, he broke a bowl. But he always caught the birds. He put them in punctured cartons for us and we fed them bread and *garri*. The birds died after a day or two. One lasted four days, and when, finally, it died, Fide held its rigid feathery form in his hand and said, joking, "It's in the sky now, asking God for bread." Years later, after Fide died, I would think about this: a bird raising a stiff wing to ask God for bread.

My mother often shouted at Fide. She was creative with her Igbo insults. "You are a fat millipede, *nnukwu esu!*" she'd say when he took too long with a task. "Look at him, *ike akpi*, with the buttocks of a scorpion," when he forgot yet another thing she'd asked him to do. Or, "May dogs lick your eyes!" when he didn't tell the truth. She asked Fide to start dinner in the afternoon because it took him so long—jollof rice alone kept him busy for four hours. One afternoon stands out in my mind. Fide was at the Formica-topped kitchen table, scraping the scales off a tilapia with a knife. He worked with slow, deliberate motions—scrape, pause, scrape, pause. There were transparent scales on his chin, on his arms, on the floor. "You're taking forever to do that!" I said. "It's like preparing a body for a funeral," Fide said. "You take your time to do it well." It was a joke, and he was laughing. But, after he died, I would think about this, too.

Fide was enrolled in a commercial school, the Universal Secretarial Academy, a grand name for a small building that had four rooms and rusty typewriters, and a grander

abbreviation. On his schoolbooks, beneath "Fide Abonyi," Fide wrote, in bold, proud letters, "U.S.A."

When my brothers borrowed videotapes of British and American films from friends, Fide watched them with us. When we borrowed books from the library, Fide would hold them and move his lips. When there were military coups in far-away Lagos, my father placed the radio on the dining table and Fide joined us as we crowded around and listened to announcements spoken in English with a northern Nigerian accent, interspersed with stretches of melancholy martial music. The coup in 1993 happened on a blustery Harmattan day. General Sani Abacha had taken over the government. "Fellow Nigerians," he began, and already we were numb. Coup announcements made you numb: the choicelessness, the fact that you were being told just for your information, just so that you would not be surprised to see a different portrait on the walls of airports and government offices.

Because there was nothing you could do about it.

It was the custom to "start a life" for your houseboy or housegirl, after he or she had been with you long enough. Fide was with us for twelve years. When my parents asked him what he wanted to do after he left us, they hoped that he would want to continue his secretarial studies. But Fide wanted to join the Army, and did so.

At first, he wrote excited letters, and sent pictures of himself in camouflage holding a long, gleaming gun. He took special pride in his boots and wrote about how he polished them with Kiwi polish, the way he had polished the shoes my father wore to his lectures. His handwriting was barely legible and his English was comic. "Hungry is killing me," he said. He wrote about the poor state of the barracks. He wrote about not being paid. Slowly, the letters cooled. Then, in a hasty letter, he wrote that he might be sent to Liberia, as part of the Nigerian Peacekeeping Force.

Civil war was raging there. People were being skinned alive, he wrote. People were being dragged to their deaths.

"He won't go to Liberia," my father said. "He'll be fine."

Fide did not go to Liberia. Months later, a military coup took place in Sierra Leone. And General Sani Abacha, who routinely killed activists, who routinely shut down the media, who routinely jailed opponents, decided to send in Nigerian troops to restore democracy.

When my parents told me that Fide had died—he was blown up by a land mine in Sierra Leone, on September 3, 1997—I stared at them for a while and then started to smile because I knew that they were wrong.

"Which Fide?" I asked, as if he were not the only Fide we knew.

"Our own Fide," my mother said, and those words will never leave me, because even as grief enveloped me I realized how lovely they were. Our own Fide. He was our own.

Fide's Jollof Rice

2 medium tomatoes, chopped finely (or substitute a small can of crushed tomatoes)

½ medium Scotch bonnet pepper (or use a habanero pepper), stem removed

3 small red bell peppers, chopped

1 ½ teaspoons salt

freshly ground pepper to taste

½ cup groundnut oil or olive oil

½ large yellow onion, chopped (about 1 ⅓ cups)

1 teaspoon Nigerian curry powder

1 teaspoon cayenne powder

2 bay leaves

1 tablespoon dried thyme

1 cup chicken or beef broth, plus more as needed

2 ½ cups medium-grain rice

parsley, chopped as garnish (optional)

Add tomatoes and peppers to a mixer or blender and purée until smooth. Season with salt and pepper, then set aside.

In a medium-sized pot, heat your oil on medium-high heat. Then add the onions and fry them until they start to turn a golden brown. Once the onions have turned golden, pour in the blended tomato and pepper sauce, cook for a few minutes, then add the curry powder, cayenne powder, bay leaves, thyme, and chicken or beef broth. Bring this mixture to a low boil, then reduce heat to low.

Add the rice and mix well.

Cover the pot so that the rice steams and doesn't burn while the sauce gets absorbed. Stir occasionally and let it simmer on low heat. After 25 minutes, check on the rice: if there's still a lot of sauce, remove the lid to prevent burning; if it's dry, add more broth.

When the liquid has mostly dried up, stir once more, then turn off the heat and let the rice sit for 10 minutes to finish cooking.

Garnish with parsley and serve alongside peppery tilapia, fried plantains, and coleslaw.

SACK LUNCH

DON LEE

Don Lee is the author of the novels *Lonesome Lies Before Us*, *The Collective*, *Wrack and Ruin*, and *Country of Origin*, and the story collection *Yellow*. He teaches in the MFA program in creative writing at Temple University.

My mother died young—when she was fifty-nine. She had a stroke while swimming in a pool and drowned. In the hospital, never having regained consciousness, she went into cardiac arrest and died. I was thirty years old.

My father and sister asked me to compose the eulogy, and what I ended up writing about were the sack lunches she used to make for me. My father had been a career State Department officer, and we were stationed overseas for most of my childhood and youth. I spent high school in Tokyo and went to an international school that was an hour and fifteen minutes outside of the city by subway and train. Every morning, my mother would wake up at 6 a.m., make my lunch, and see me out the door to catch the 6:50 subway. She did this without fail every school day for four years.

A typical sack lunch included two homemade chicken salad sandwiches, sticks of carrots and celery, cookies, potato chips, and an orange. The meal was not at all fancy, but it was lovingly, meticulously prepared—so much so, that sometimes the packages of food seemed too flawless, too precious in themselves, to disturb, much less eat. This was exemplified by the orange. She would slice the outer skin so it would open up like the petals of a flower, still connected at the base. She would peel off the inner white membrane of the orange, then put it back—now pristine and tender—into its protective skin.

My mother displayed this habit of perfection and dedication in everything she did. She tried to spoil us rotten, making these lunches, serving snacks and desserts, cooking all the meals. Yet she was not, in truth, a very good cook. Neither was I at the time of her death.

All in all, it was a terrible year. For months, whenever I was in public, I would be afraid of breaking out in sobs, as I was on the verge of doing whenever I thought about my mother. Also: My girlfriend cheated on me, and we broke up. The IRS nailed me for two thousand dollars for failing to pay all my self-employment tax, when my annual income had been less than twenty thousand. Every story I submitted to magazines was rejected. I busted a bone in my foot running, and I had to stay on crutches for ten weeks. I lived in a fourth-floor walkup, and it was a hassle, a pain, to go up and down the stairs, so I

ended up trapped in my apartment, which led to making one particular meal on a regular basis. Ramen.

Specifically, it was Sapporo Ichiban packaged ramen. I would boil it with Oscar Mayer bologna that I had sliced into thin strips, cabbage, and the yolk of an egg. This sorry concoction, believe it or not, I had learned from my mother. I don't know where or from whom she had learned it. As a Korean American who had spent a lot of time in Japan, she should have been ashamed of such ramen toppings. Yet I suspect it originated when we were stationed in Seoul, Korea. We lived on the embassy housing compound next door to the Yongsan Eighth Army base, and we shopped at the PX and commissary, which was limited in what they stocked, save for Oscar Mayer bologna and cans of Campbell's soup. So she made ramen with bologna, cabbage, and egg, and omelets with pieces of bologna and green onion beaten into the egg, and chicken thighs that omitted the egg but were baked with Campbell's cream of mushroom soup poured on top. Another recipe in frequent rotation was chicken cacciatore, baked with Campbell's cream of tomato soup poured on top. The meals were bland not only in taste but also in preparation—everything spread too evenly, cut too precisely, positioned too equidistantly.

Did she get these recipes from other embassy or Army wives? Or simply from the labels on the Campbell's soup cans? I don't know. She was first generation, so she hadn't been very familiar with Western food before meeting my father. She'd grown up eating mostly Korean food, and she was better at making Asian dishes, the ramen notwithstanding. But I was fucked-up about my identity then and wanted to eat American food almost exclusively, and she tried to accommodate me as best as she could. So maybe I was largely to blame for all those nitrate-filled abominations.

I didn't really learn how to cook until long past her death, when I began hanging out with a large clan in Boston who became my surrogate family. I've spent over twenty-five Thanksgivings with them, and I've watched my friend BJ and her mother, Jane, and her siblings cook dozens of meals. The most important thing I've learned—besides that I should ditch the bologna and Campbell's—is that some spontaneity and a little swagger help you as a cook. It's not good to be too meticulous and genteel, as my mother had been (that *orange*). You should be able to look in the pantry, pick out whatever's available and fresh, and throw something together. You should also be willing to make a mess.

That's how I came up with the accompanying recipe. One summer day, BJ said, "Don, why don't you cook us lunch for a change?" I looked around the kitchen. Her mother had grown a bumper crop of zucchinis in her garden that season, and someone had grated several zucchinis to make zucchini bread later. I confiscated them for our lunch, and the dish was born—a light, fresh summertime pasta that, despite its simple ingredients, was long on subtle flavor. BJ's nieces named it "Sweetie Zucchini Linguine Fini," and it has become—no offense to you, Mom—a family favorite.

Sweetie Zucchini Linguine Fini

3 zucchinis
salt
¾ pound linguine fini
4 tablespoons extra-virgin
 olive oil
4 to 5 garlic cloves,
 minced

½ onion, sliced thin
red pepper flakes
black pepper
herbs (thyme or rosemary)
Parmesan cheese, grated, at
 least ½ cup
walnuts, crushed

Grate the zucchinis and put them in a colander, then sprinkle with salt. Sweat them for 20 minutes or so.

Bring a large pot of salted water to a boil and begin cooking the linguine fini.

Heat at least 3 tablespoons of olive oil in a large sauté pan; add the garlic and onion and a dash of red pepper flakes.

Drain the linguine and add it to the pan, tossing and mixing with the garlic and onion.

Sprinkle with black pepper and whatever herbs you have (e.g., thyme, rosemary) and toss.

Squeeze water out of the zucchini and then mix it into the linguine. Toss with Parmesan and a handful of crushed walnuts. (If you only have whole walnuts, put them in a Ziploc and bang with the bottom of a jar.)

Slide the linguine into a serving bowl, drizzle with a bit of olive oil, and top with a sprinkling of Parmesan and walnuts to taste.

MERENGUITOS

CHANTEL ACEVEDO

Chantel Acevedo is the author of *Love and Ghost Letters*; *A Falling Star*; *The Distant Marvels*, which was a finalist for the 2016 Andrew Carnegie Medal for Excellence in Fiction; and most recently, *The Living Infinite*, hailed by *Booklist* as a "vivid and enthralling tale of love and redemption." Her essays have appeared in *Vogue* and *Real Simple*, among other publications. She is an associate professor of English at the University of Miami, where she teaches in the MFA program.

My mother fell in love with un Americano the same year my grandfather got sick and I turned thirteen. It was a year of many changes. For one thing, we all had to grow used to this new man in the house, a tall gringo with blond hair and blue eyes, who played golf, rooted for Notre Dame, and said things like, "Take a Louie," when he meant "Go left." He listened to the Eagles, had a redheaded sister and a towheaded brother, and came from upstate New York, where he once took a hockey puck to the head, which knocked out his sense of smell forever.

My abuelo called him "el Yanqui" to his face, adopting the language of communist Cuba, even though he'd left the island in 1953, well before Fidel. It was strange for my grandfather, a man of decorum and softness, to take such an aggressive position on anybody, even a man dating his daughter. It was the first clue that something was not right with my grandfather.

The more confused and difficult my grandfather became, the more my grandmother had to tend to him. She took up a permanent spot in the front parlor, la sala, as we called it, making sure her husband didn't escape. My grandfather had already sold some of her jewelry at the pharmacy down the street for five dollars and she often caught him with more valuables in his pocket, mingling with his forbidden car keys. By the time el Yanqui moved in, having officially become my stepfather, we had a temporary name for my grandfather's condition—dementia.

Before Abuelo got sick, he would come home from the body shop where he worked carrying one of those old-fashioned black tin lunchboxes, placing it on the kitchen counter with a soft clink. Home in time for merienda, my abuela always had a pot of vegetable soup—calabaza, boniato, plátanos— bubbling on the stove for him. She ladled big spoonfuls into his bowl, while he sat at the counter and slurped loudly, murmuring into the steam, reaching out to caress his wife now and again, a woman he called "Nena." It was his nickname for her, one no other person in the world used. My grandfather would then change into an undershirt and fresh jeans and putter around in the backyard, tending to his avocado tree, the banana plants, and the sour lemon tree that grew lumpy lemons the size of my head. He would pick up fallen mangoes from the ground, fertilize the tamarindo tree, or straighten the tall papayas, which always reminded me of Dr. Seuss's truffula trees, so lanky and fluffy at the top. Our backyard was a fruit-lover's heaven, the bounty of which often made it back into the kitchen for creamy batidos made in the blender, or else, my abuelo would take bushels of fruit to work and give them away to men who peeled it with oil-blackened hands. Dinner was served before the sun came down, with a telenovela blaring in the background. A big pot of rice, the ever-present beans, with chicken, or cubed beef, or picadillo. The air was all garlic and onion. The cabinets were sticky with oil, as were the beaded curtains that divided the dining room from the Florida room. But the tile floors gleamed—mopped with lavender-scented Mistolin after dinner every night.

Some evenings, the dishes still piled high in the sink, my grandmother would invite me into the kitchen at last. This was a big deal. The kitchen was my abuela's domain, so much so that she never taught my mother to cook, and shooed me out of the kitchen whenever I turned up in there. Often, she'd point to the pressure cooker. "Un peligro," she'd say, the ch-ch-ch-ch of the pot making up the rhythm of my life, the beans inside the staple of our diet. I eyed it with suspicion, wondering what made it so dangerous. Stepping into her kitchen felt like an invitation to something beyond the grandmother-granddaughter relationship. It felt like friendship. She would hand me two eggs, and produce two bowls—one for the whites, one for the yolks. My job was to separate the whites, put in the sugar and vanilla. The rest was up to her. With a fork, just a fork,

"One day, the pressure cooker did, indeed, explode."

~ Chantel Acevedo

she would whip up the eggs until they formed peaks. She was a tiny woman, but so strong. I imagined she could make tornadoes out of thin air with that fork. Then, she'd fire up a burner on the stove, pierce a little cloud of whipped eggs with the fork, and hold it over the burner, toasting the merenguito just right. They would turn out brown on the edges, and nothing like the ones that came in bags at the bodega. It was our version of a campfire, I guess, and the only time I was allowed in the kitchen. We would eat the merenguitos in silence, punctuated sometimes with my abuela telling me, "Te quiero, Chantel. Cuanto te quiero," which, in that moment, I knew more certainly than anything else in the world.

It all changed so quickly. One minute, my life was the same as it ever was. My mom, abuelo, abuela, and I made a perfect quartet, a Cuban machine that hummed along the days, cycling through the year, holidays and birthdays, punctuated by visits from Cuban relatives, my grandmother's siblings, nieces and nephews, exiles all, who stared at the cupboards in fascination, and who hoarded food under their fold-out beds until they learned that there was enough, no rations here.

The next minute, my abuelo was looking at me as if he didn't recognize me anymore, or picking me up from school and getting lost on the way home. My grandfather, that gentle person, was the first naked man I ever saw. He'd emerged dripping wet from a shower without a shred of clothes on, headed straight to the front door of the house, and tried to leave. My grandmother fought him, slippery as he was. He overpowered her, but somehow, when the warmth of the day outside hit his skin, he relented, turned around, and asked about dinner. But his appetite was gone. The backyard trees were ignored. By dinnertime, when he was "sun-downing," the term given to Alzheimer's patients' late-in-the-day confusion, my grandparents would take themselves to bed while my mother, stepfather, and I ate the meal my grandmother had prepared. El Yanqui would parse out the beans, leaving them on the side of his plate. "I only eat the baked kinds," he'd say, meaning the ones that came in a can, soaked in that brown syrup.

One day, the pressure cooker did, indeed, explode. The lid flew off the top like a missile, cracking a cabinet in half. Luckily, the kitchen had been empty, but the violence of the moment paired with the violence of my grandfather's illness meant that my grandmother was done in the kitchen for good.

My mother took over, swapping out beans and rice for spaghetti, carne con papa for lamb chops and apple sauce, a dish which I thought only existed on episodes of *The Brady Bunch*, but which my new stepfather ate with relish. My mother was a terrible cook, pushed out of the kitchen by my grandmother all those years. She had no innate sense of how flavors might come together. I have inherited this disorder, having once decorated a chocolate cake with grapes. But this is not about me. My mother learned to make the bland foods that my stepfather liked so much, the food that reminded him of home, of his Irish Canadian mother who collected Belleek chinaware and copper molds and made desserts out of Jell-O. Lynyrd Skynyrd would sometimes be playing in the background while we ate, the telenovelas and their manufactured drama having been removed from the evening lineup. My grandmother, picking at her plate, would mutter, "Esto no es comida," as if the food in front of her was only pretending to be edible.

It wasn't long before things had to change again. My grandfather, no longer continent, no longer intelligible most days, increasingly violent, had to go away. The night they took him to the nursing home was the first time I'd ever been left alone in the house. I gave my grandfather a hug at the door, an embrace he didn't return. Instead, he took it like a telephone pole, his eyes glassy and already gone.

For fifteen years he lived in that home—speechless, bedridden, his muscles curling in on themselves, his tongue twisting and hardening like cured sausage. For fifteen years, because as the doctors cruelly pointed out, "he had the heart of a young man," my grandmother spent every day at his side, feeding him meals off of plastic trays, mashed, unidentifiable things. She would come back at night smelling of the home, and she would eat leftovers of things like Salisbury steak with carrots and peas, or meatloaf, and it didn't matter really, because sustenance and survival were the same thing now. It was harder to remember him as different from this fragile shell of a person as my teenage years rolled on. When I was little, I used to sit on his lap, and he would scratch my back with hard, calloused fingers. I remember, too, how he held baby banana plants in the cup of his hand, transferring them away from the mother plant, giving her room to continue to grow. It was hard to remember my grandmother, too, the lightness in her eyes, how she used to sing "Don't Cry for Me Argentina," with hidden heartache in her voice.

Some nights, however, when Abuelo had gone to sleep early, and when the Miami traffic was light on the way home, she'd call me into the kitchen, her once-domain, with two eggs in hand. "Ven aca, mi vida," she would say, her sweet tooth and mine beckoning, the hurricane strength in her arm winding up, whipping, frothing, making sweetness out of what was bitter and hard to swallow.

Los Merenguitos de Nena

SERVES 2

2 egg whites
½ cup of granulated sugar
5 drops of vanilla extract

Beat eggs with a fork* until frothy, then slowly add the sugar and vanilla extract. Continue beating the eggs with a fork until stiff peaks form.

Then, swirl the fork in the mixture until a Ping-Pong-ball-sized clump clings to the fork. Hold the fork and mixture over a stovetop† set on medium, being careful not to burn yourself. Twist the fork until the merenguito hardens. The edges will be brown, but the inside will be gooey like marshmallow.

Eat it off the fork.

---

* You can also use a mixer if you're in a hurry, or don't have my abuela's hurricane arm-strength.
† Most people bake their merenguitos the way one makes cookies, setting them on parchment paper and putting them in a preheated oven at 200°F for an hour and a half.

A GRAIN OF COMFORT

EDWIDGE DANTICAT

Edwidge Danticat is the author of several books, including *Breath, Eyes, Memory*, an Oprah's Book Club selection; *Krik? Krak!*, a National Book Award finalist; *The Farming of Bones*, an American Book Award winner; and the novel-in-stories *The Dew Breaker*. She has written six books for young adults and children, as well as a travel narrative; her memoir, *Brother, I'm Dying*, was a 2007 finalist for the National Book Award and a 2008 winner of the National Book Critics Circle Award for autobiography. Her next book, *Everything Inside*, will be published by Knopf in August 2019.

I had no idea it would be our last meal together. My father, ill with pulmonary fibrosis for a year and bedridden for nine months, told me he wanted a bowl of plain white rice for supper. A staple of our family's Haitian diet, rice was something we consumed nearly every day. Early in his illness, however, he had decided firmly, if incorrectly, that rice grains were contributing to his clogged lungs and aggravating his agonizing cough, so he abruptly stopped eating them.

Overjoyed that my father was actually craving something other than the nutritional supplement Ensure that comprised most of his meals, I rushed to share the news with my mother.

My mother was my father's sole around-the-clock caregiver. She'd watched him shrink from 170 pounds down to 90 and was the first to hold his hand when he lost the ability to walk by himself. And the afternoon he longed for rice, she was the only person he would allow to cook it for him.

She immediately sent me back to ask my father exactly how he wanted his rice prepared. Could she soak it in chicken broth, mix it with black or brown beans or mushrooms, sprinkle it with shredded cashews? Would he mind if she lubricated it with butter or margarine to add some extra calories and taste, if she stirred in chunks of sausage or bacon for much-needed protein? Perhaps he wanted some fresh vegetables thrown in for fiber?

I rushed back upstairs to what had been my parents' bedroom and was now his alone, the queen-size bed replaced by a buzzing oxygen machine and narrow hospital bed that allowed my father to prop himself up at the push of a button to reply that he wanted only a small bowl of the plainest white rice my mother could possibly prepare. He even provided a shorthand recipe: "Cup of rice, water, drop of salt, spoonful of vegetable oil. Boil it all together."

My father had always been a picky eater. When he left Haiti and moved to the United States in 1971, he was forced to come without my mother because she couldn't obtain a visa. The meals he prepared for himself as a suddenly exiled bachelor always included meat, usually chicken or pork; some boiled plantains; and inevitably rice. When my mother was able to join him two years later, the first thing he did was cook her a lavish Sunday meal of stewed chicken, fried plantains, and rice and beans. Each time someone would visit from Haiti, my father would cook that same meal—his welcome repast, he called it—because he wanted his guests to taste what had buffered his transition to immigrant life. And even if their stays would not be as long as his, he hoped they would feel, as he did, that one could easily return home simply by lifting a fork to one's lips.

I watched silently as my mother prepared my father's rice. When she dropped the contents of an overflowing measuring cup into a pot of boiling water, a few grains spilled out, turning black in the oven flames. I thought I saw her hands tremble as she lowered the lid to trap in some of the steam that would prevent the rice from becoming sticky. My father liked his rice light and fluffy, separate. Since he'd gone so long without a taste, the possibility of disappointing him weighed heavily on my mother.

When the rice was done, she searched a cabinet filled with her special-occasion dishes, the kind she used only when she had company, and pulled out a gorgeous white porcelain plate with two giant cherries sketched in the middle. The cherries overlapped in a way that made them look like one large heart, and as my mother heaped the rice on top of them, they seemed like a coded message from a woman who was beyond taking ordinary moments with her husband for granted.

I brought the rice up to my father on the bright yellow bed tray we served all his meals on. My mother added a tall glass of ice-cold water, which he'd requested at the last minute. When I walked into the room, my father's face lit up, his eyes sparkling with anticipation. He was wrapped in three heavy comforters, which were doing the

work that muscle and fat had once done for his body.

As I leaned over to place the tray in front of him, the forward sway of my body spilled the chilled water right onto his chest and lap. The water soaked through the comforters and into my father's pajamas.

My father let out a loud cry. I quickly pulled the tray aside and rested it on the dresser across from his bed. Even as he moaned and tried to wriggle away from the wet comforters, his eyes trailed the plate of rice that was now cooling off just a few feet away.

My mother heard my father's screams and hurried to his rescue. She quickly peeled back the sheets, all the while shouting for me to get her a towel and dry pajamas from the closet.

My father's pained utterances quickly went from moans to wails.

"Oh, God!" he called out tearfully. Because of his illness, he was oversensitive to the cold and must have felt as though he were being drowned in an icy lake.

My mother removed his pajamas

and patted him down with the towel. In addition to the fibrosis in his lung, my father suffered from psoriasis, which covered large portions of his skin with dried scaly patches. This was the first and only time I'd seen my father naked. Not only was his body bared but his carefully hidden lesions were, too.

An hour later, he was still shivering under three dry comforters. It took some oxygen and a nebulizer to stabilize him again. By then the rice was cold and he showed no desire for it.

"I'm sorry, Papa," I said.

"It was an accident." He raised one bony hand from under the blankets to grab mine. "I know you didn't mean to do it."

"I ruined the rice for you," I said. "I know how much you wanted it."

He hesitated, then pressed my hand harder.

"I didn't want it so much as I wanted to want it," he said. "The truth is, I don't feel hungry or thirsty anymore. I just wish I did."

It pained me much more to hear this than to hear him saying the day before that he'd dreamed of long-dead relatives standing at his bedside. It pained me more than the way he introduced nearly every sentence with "When I'm gone." I remembered being angry at him the previous Thanksgiving when he surveyed the feast at our family dinner table and curtly declared, "There's nothing here I can eat." After cooking for two days, my mother had been devastated. What we didn't know, however, and what my father himself had no idea of at the time, was that the disease was slowly eating away at his body's yearning for food and quickly wiping out his reliance on it.

Sitting with him that night after the water spill, holding his hand, I could smell it before we saw it—a new batch of long-grain white rice prepared by my mother. This time she brought it up herself, and not on the bed tray but on a round silver server from the special cabinet. My father raised himself on the bed to receive it, and as soon as my mother handed him the spoon—for he always ate his rice with a spoon—he immediately dove in. He barely chewed at all, simply bouncing the grains from cheek to cheek, then swallowing quickly. Had I not known, I would have thought him famished, ravenous, even insatiable. And perhaps he was. Or maybe he was desperately trying to nourish himself with something recognizable and familiar.

When he was halfway done, my father handed me the plate.

"Do you want some?" he asked.

"There's more in the kitchen," my mother said. "She can have it later. This is for you."

"Let her have some," he insisted.

I reached over and took the plate. Using my father's spoon, I piled a mound of rice into my mouth. It was plain but flavorful, delicious. I suspected that my mother might have slipped in some broth or margarine, even a few drops of coconut milk, but I couldn't be sure.

Handing the rest of the rice back to my father, I said, "Thank you, Papa."

Three days later, my father was dead. In the interim, he'd stopped eating altogether.

I will always be grateful I shared that plate of rice with my father because for nearly a year my mother, my brothers, and I had constantly brought him food yet had rarely eaten with him. Somehow it hadn't occurred to us that he missed sharing a table or a dish, passing a spice or a spoon. But he did.

Three weeks before he died, my parents had their fortieth wedding anniversary. My brothers and I invited a few friends over, even though my father was too weak to leave his bed. Still, as we all gathered around, he seemed relieved for once to be at the center of an occasion that did not involve his illness. The simple act of rejoicing, our honoring the day he and my mother were married, he said, allowed him to momentarily concentrate on life rather than death. And even the simplest life, like the simplest meal, is cause for celebration.

Diri Blan (White Rice)

2 cups water
1 tablespoon vegetable oil
2 tablespoons coconut
   milk (optional)

1 tablespoon salt
1 cup white rice

In a saucepan over medium heat, bring water, oil, and coconut milk (if using) to a boil. Add salt and rice. Reduce heat to low and cook covered until water is completely absorbed, about 25 minutes. Grains should be tender and separate.

WHAT I ATE

NICK FLYNN

Nick Flynn has worked as a ship's captain, as an electrician, and as a caseworker with homeless adults. Recent books include *Stay*, a collection of collaborations and writings, and *I Will Destroy You*, a collection of poems. Flynn's film credits include executive producer and artistic collaborator on *Being Flynn*, the film version of his memoir *Another Bullshit Night in Suck City*. Currently he is a professor on the creative writing faculty at the University of Houston, where he is in residence each spring. His work has been translated into fifteen languages.

Yesterday I wrote the words *doctor appointment* in the log in the principal's office at my daughter's elementary school. I stood at the front desk, the log open in front of me. I considered writing the truth—*sometimes my daughter and I just get in the car and drive.* The log, though, made it clear that every other child from her classroom who'd skipped out of school early that month (there weren't many) had been pulled out because of a doctor appointment. I considered writing *restlessness*, but instead simply copied the entry before mine.

The truth is I was due to talk on a panel the next morning at a poetry festival. My wife was out of town, our childcare had fallen through, so my daughter and I were taking the Megabus to Boston. My friend Tom had told me that The Breeders were playing that night, and he had access to a couple tickets. The Breeders! Kim Deal! Kelley Deal!

Josephine Wiggs! A supergroup of grrrrl power! How could I deny my ten-year-old daughter this, her first rock concert?

The bus ride was supposed to take four hours, but it ended up taking over five. We passed the time. We did a few exquisite corpses, we read a little, we looked out the window. We watched a disc of *Beasts of the Southern Wild*, which, as you know, is narrated by a six-year-old girl.

At first, I'd pause the disc every few minutes to transcribe a bit of evocative dialogue onto my phone:

The whole universe depends on everything fitting together just right . . . if one piece busts, even the smallest piece, the entire universe will get busted . . .

This idea of the universe breaking began to thread through the film:

The entire universe depends on everything fitting together just right . . . if you can fix the broken piece, everything can go right back . . .

It echoed alongside the idea that something can be broken beyond repair:

Sometimes you can break something so bad it can't go back together.

A lot of things were breaking on the screen—things were thrown, guns were shot, a trailer set on fire. The ice shelf was melting; prehistoric beasts were set loose in the swamps. A storm was coming. At one point my daughter took the phone from me and began taking notes herself:

When you small you got fix what you can.

What she heard was different than what I heard. Her notes showed me something inside her that I hadn't yet glimpsed.

I gotta get strong.

I yanked her out of school one day a couple years ago and we took the A train to Coney Island. She was seven years old then, she'd lived in Brooklyn her whole life, and she'd never been to Coney Island. What kind of father was I? We rode on a few rides, put our feet in the ocean, gave some money to the carnies, ate a hot dog. She doesn't even remember that day, but I have to believe it is somewhere inside her, lurking in her cells.

On these trips I always bring a sack of food—Clif bars, veggie chips, chocolate, apples, clementines. As we watched the film we ate our way through it. The father in *Beasts of the Southern Wild* was both dying and a drunk. He always had a whole chicken waiting in a cooler; at dinnertime he'd stick it with a big fork and throw it onto a grill. He wasn't what you'd call a good father—verbally abusive, physically abusive—but he stuck around until he died. He was teaching his daughter how to survive.

Here are a few recipes from *Beasts of the Southern Wild*:

a whole chicken from a
    cooler, forked onto a grill
cat food mixed with canned
    gravy, sautéed in a big pot
a crawfish / crab boil
a catfish, caught by hand
    and punched in the head

The Megabus makes one stop, halfway through, at a gas station. We were told we had fifteen minutes to pee and get more food. It reminded me of a time in my life when gas stations were the only place I'd eat. At the time this phase seemed endless. It lasted about a year, though it might have been two. It was the year after my mother died, and for a while it seemed every sunrise would find me asleep in my car. It was a year I always seemed to be driving, but I didn't get anywhere. I was a vegetarian when she died so I figured I should remain a vegetarian after she died. I was living on coffee, smoking a lot of pot, both of which I thought of as types of food.

Here's the recipe:

1 pound of coffee
1 bag of marijuana
a lighter (matches will do)

I was living in Massachusetts, not far from where I was born. I was working on a boat, which was on land, trying to get it ready to go in the water. The plan was to live on it once—if—I got it floating. It would be my home. It was raised into the air on jacks. I was putting in twelve-hour days. Most nights I'd end up falling asleep on it, which was better than sleeping in my car. When I woke I'd make a pot of oatmeal. If I had raisins or nuts or maple syrup I'd add them, but I usually only had the oats, if that.

Here's the recipe:

2 cups of water
1 cup of oats

Boil the water, add the oats. Let it simmer until a spoon can stand up in it. Add whatever else is lying around.

My daughter pauses the disc:

Everybody loses the thing that made them . . . it's even how it's supposed to be in nature.

The days were getting short, the sun was going down. I had so much to learn. I wasn't much of a carpenter, and even if I were, a carpenter is not a boat-builder. Another day slipped inside itself and I was, at that time, feral. Regular people, civilians, turned away from me. Now the sun was down, and I'd forgotten to eat, again. I could make more oatmeal but I knew I should get out. I hadn't spoken to a soul all day. The nearest place was a gas station, the nearest place is always a gas station. The lights were on, inside was well-lit. I was a vegetarian, so I avoided the Slim Jims. I went to the chip aisle, got a big bag. I can't remember which brand, I didn't have a brand. Then I got a container of cottage cheese. I sat in my car in the parking lot, dipping the chips, one by one, into the cottage cheese, until both were gone.

Here's the recipe:

1 large bag of potato chips
1 container of cottage
  cheese

My daughter pauses the disc:

When it all goes quiet behind
my eyes I see everything
that made me, flying around
in invisible pieces. When I
look too hard, it goes away.
But when it all goes quiet, I
see they are right here. I see
that I'm a little piece of a big,
big universe, and that makes
things right. When I die,
the scientists of the future,
they're gonna find it all.

Healing

JULIA'S STEPCHILD

EMILY RABOTEAU

Emily Raboteau's books are *The Professor's Daughter* and *Searching for Zion*, winner of an American Book Award. Other distinctions include a Pushcart Prize, the *Chicago Tribune's* Nelson Algren Award, and fellowships from NEA, NYFA, and the Lannan Foundation. Her short fiction and essays have been widely published in such places as *The New Yorker*, *The New York Times*, *The Believer*, *McSweeney's*, *Freeman's*, *The Guardian*, and *Guernica*. She teaches creative writing at The City College of New York, in Harlem.

Before my father left his second wife for his third, Julia made me congee. I was twenty-six, living in New York, at the violent end of the relationship with the alcoholic I started dating in high school. It didn't matter that I'd been the one to do the leaving—my sense of abandonment, loneliness, and heartache was nearly as profound as my mother's had been when my father split. My mother, whom I'd mercilessly judged for being weak.

I couldn't get it together after the breakup. I lost my appetite along with my sense of self and shrank to eighty-nine pounds. The skeletal young woman in the mirror repulsed me. I reminded myself of my mother, at her nadir. Gutted, I wanted only to sleep, or die. A therapist recommended antidepressants.

Julia's saving cure was congee. She understood I couldn't digest anything else. I needed the most basic, pre-masticated food, food for the toothless, food that would stick to my bones. She showed me how to fill the pot with the correct proportion of water and jasmine rice, and then stayed for hours until the fragrant smell filled my messy apartment. She added minced ginger and chopped scallions for taste. She sat with me and watched me eat it.

DURING THE COURSE OF MY parents' very public divorce it bothered me that people openly assumed my black father had left my white mother for a black woman, as if race was the obvious problem in their marriage. Julia (also white) was tall, bony, and big-nosed, with an unruly cloud of white hair, odd clothes, and slight jowls. Bucking stereotype, she was older than my dad. Yet somehow she'd seduced him. She emanated a kind of shamanistic power with her dancer's posture and homeopathy. My superficial first impression at sixteen was that she resembled a witch.

Is there anyone more maligned in children's stories than the step-mother? But I didn't actually see Julia as wicked. Nobody who'd seen her at work as an art therapist could accuse her of that. As a teenager, I saw her as something worse—buffoonish. She struck me in her hand-stitched hemp tunics and Birkenstocks as an aging hippie who worshipped Chinese medicine and spent too much money on deodorant made of rock salt; a failed conceptual artist whose aesthetic aped Basquiat's New York *Downtown 81* vibe; a do-gooder whose care for the black poor I suspected of cultural envy, paternalism, and white liberal guilt. It was impossible to love her in the beginning. I was loyal enough to my mother that the only aspect of Julia's character to escape my early criticism was her cuisine.

Julia's cooking tended to be vegan and macrobiotic; I still crave it like certain pregnant women crave dirt. Roasted root vegetables and squash, brown rice, wilted winter greens, toasted nuts, slow-cooked beans, seasonal vegetables, and healthier versions of Southern dishes she'd grown up on in North Carolina—corn bread, sweet potato pie, black-eyed peas. She cultivated most of the fresh ingredients in the garden. Anyone who ever enjoyed a meal at Angelica Kitchen (Julia's favorite restaurant) on the Lower East Side before it closed in 2017 will understand the alchemy that made this food good. You could taste the earthy love that went into its preparation. As with the congee she would later introduce me to, it was simple, and took time. I couldn't get enough of it, even as I begrudged the other guests at the dining table edging in on my broken family. These were Julia's people.

WHEN MY FATHER MET HER IN the mid-nineties, Julia was running an art-clinic in East Harlem for the mentally ill, some of whom lived occasionally on the street. She didn't call them mentally ill, or homeless, but "clients." The clinic, Souls-in-Motion, was a vast basement space attached to a daytime psychiatric rehabilitation center. She'd transformed the underground realm with swaths of fabric, reclaimed furniture, rescued animals, found objects, potted plants, and art supplies into a fantabulous art studio and gallery. There were separate workstations for writing, sewing, basket-weaving, stretching, painting, making, and communing. The enterprise was so well-lit, dynamic, and artfully decorated that you forgot not only that it was a basement but that it was a room with walls. In the adjacent lot grew a community garden that Julia also maintained, equally abundant and wild.

The art on display was uninhibited and terrifically strange—the projections of blazing minds. There were intentionally ugly ragdolls, abstract quilts, life-size portraits done entirely with Crayola markers, zany totems of stained scrap wood: part dinosaur, part piano. Souls-in-Motion reminded me in spirit of *Pee-wee's Playhouse*. I probably made that association because back when she was productive as an artist in her own right Julia had designed, of all things, the jeweled box containing the head of Jambi the Genie. Souls-in-Motion was as playful as that TV show. The community's ragtag crew included a giant African leopard tortoise, a one-eyed stray cat, and a rabbit called Jack. There were hammocks for the artists to sleep off their meds when they weren't actively making; desks and drafting tables made of discarded doors for them to work at, beneath which the animals freely wandered.

My father and Julia held their wedding reception at Souls-in-Motion. It was something like the Mad Hatter's tea party. I remember getting knocked down by an elder wearing a ripped pink satin dress as she maniacally chased after the rabbit with a broom, her wig askew, her face smeared with frosting from the homemade wedding cake. That lady was Doris, one of the clients who became a regular guest at the house my father and Julia now shared.

Watching Julia's gracious interactions with Doris and the other clients over time, I came to appreciate my stepmother's gift for kindness. She didn't distinguish between normal and abnormal behavior; high and low art; them and us. She was unafraid to sit next to trauma, even when it sometimes smelled. Also, there was a spiritual dimension to her socialism. Once, I heard an angry man with a single matted dreadlock that reached all the way down his back rant at her for what felt like hours. With great paranoia, hostility, and pain he decried the system that enabled her to enjoy shelter and money while keeping him endangered and oppressed. He made perfect sense while talking crazy. Julia listened receptively, calmly, to his looping monologue where most white people I know would have felt cornered, threatened, frustrated, or blamed; then she said that she was sorry, offered him a hug, fed him soup, and asked him what he wished to draw. The answer, of course, was monsters, and they were wonderful.

When I asked Julia how she was able to remain so unruffled by this man and other clients whose behavior could sometimes be rash and off-putting, she said she was attuned to what they were really saying: *Love me, love me; I didn't get the love that I deserved.* We're all expressing the same refrain at different frequencies, she explained. I believe she was right about that.

Within a year of my parents' divorce, my mother began appearing at Julia's table. I'm sure it was Julia who invited her to my father's new house. I thought it was weird to celebrate holidays together as if our family were intact until enough holidays had passed that it wasn't weird anymore. Against the odds, and to both of their credit, my mother and Julia became friends. They had a shared gift for caretaking that was expressed differently in each. I left home for college and returned at Thanksgiving and Christmas expecting, admiring, and enjoying my kooky stepmother's all-embracing hospitality. By the time I graduated, five years into her partnership with my father, I could freely admit that I loved her.

WHEN I NEEDED NOURISHING IN the wake of my breakup, Julia started with congee. Then she brought me to Chinatown and connected me to an acupuncturist she'd learned from, a woman who listened to me describe my symptoms, took my pulse, attempted to redirect my blocked energy, and prescribed herbs. What's more, Julia encouraged me to get a dog, and to write. She knitted me a pair of fingerless gloves. She had me identify colors that made me happy in ordinary objects I treasured—the sea-foam patina of an old jewelry box, the peachy brown of a flower pot, the grassy green of the fern in the pot—and helped me repaint my walls in those tones.

While we painted, Julia spoke reverently of the cracking plaster canvas of my old apartment's walls. She said its contours made it more interesting to work with than perfectly skim-coated drywall. Her technique was to use brushes instead of rollers, for the more tactile experience and textured effect. Applied this way, the walls attained a soft, pearly glow until they appeared to breathe. She pointed out how the colors changed with the angle of sunlight, and I saw what she meant. Pain had a purpose. Like a dark basement, or a fistful of rice, it could be converted with energy into something else.

Her therapeutic formulas took more time than Prozac, but worked. Five years after Julia helped me through that difficult period, I found myself in a better place—physically, financially, and emotionally—planning my wedding to a good man. That's when Julia called with the news that my father was kicking her to the curb. Just as I was finding balance, my dear stepmother was losing hers.

During their separation, Julia fell down the basement stairs, martyr to the cause. Exhaustion must have played a part. Evidently, Julia had lain prostrate for hours alone on the basement floor after the fall. *Who will take care of her?* my stepsister implored.

Not me. I admired Julia's generosity of spirit. I'd come to respect my mother's grace under fire for having to revise her family. But I couldn't sacrifice myself in their mutual way. I'm ashamed to say, I turned away. By the time Julia tumbled down the stairs she was no longer my stepmother, and I was a mother myself—preoccupied by my infant, short on sleep and compassion, I used the demands of my new family as an excuse. I'm ashamed to say I never made congee for Julia, who was my family, too.

Shame is a worthless emotion, a married lover told me once. He said it with such conviction that I believed him. Now that I'm a mother, I think differently about the value of shame, just as I think differently about the vocation of nurture. Shame is worth paying attention to. It teaches us when we're lacking an ingredient required by those who depend upon us. That ingredient is nurture, in my case—one of the most overlooked and undervalued kinds of labor. Usually, it's women's work. Julia is brilliant at it. I am not.

In the end, it was my mother who cared for Julia when she fell. The sophistication of this gesture comes as no surprise, knowing her as I do. I don't believe schadenfreude was a motivating factor. It was just my mother's way of returning a kindness.

I wonder what they talked about, my two mothers. Probably us, the children they'd parented, and him, the husband they'd shared. His shortcomings and charms. I envision Julia changing her arnica poultice; my mother offering to make her bed. I imagine that they ate.

Whatever communion they shared that afternoon belongs to them alone. I consider it sanctified and beyond my reach. Afterward, my mother arrived at my place to help with the baby. I asked her sheepishly how Julia was faring in the aftermath of her fall. This is what my mother told me, and she may just as well have been speaking for herself:

The fall was hard. It laid her low. She was floored by pain. In her way, she prayed. She contemplated her injury and surroundings at the foot of the stairs. Time passed. She figured out that none of her bones were broken. And so, remembering the people who needed her, she got up and climbed the basement stairs.

CONGEE IS EASY ENOUGH TO cook, only slightly more demanding than toast. It falls in the family of comfort-mush including oatmeal, polenta, farina, and grits. Sometimes referred to in the U.S. as the Chinese version of porridge, congee is eaten in many Asian countries for breakfast: six parts water or broth to one part rice: slow cook over low heat. I will always think of it as healing food, and it will always remind me of Julia. This is the recipe that she taught me.

Congee

6 cups water or vegetable stock
1 cup jasmine rice, rinsed
½ teaspoon salt (more to taste)
1 knob of ginger, peeled and
　thinly sliced

¼ cup sliced scallions, for
　garnish
pepper (optional)
sesame seed oil (optional)

In large pot, add vegetable stock or water, jasmine rice, salt, and ginger. Bring it to a boil and stir.

Once boiling, reduce the heat to low and allow the congee to simmer with the lid on for about an hour until it thickens, stirring occasionally (it will thicken even more once it cools). Season with additional salt and pepper to taste.

Serve hot, topped with sliced scallions and sesame oil.

NON-ALCOHOLIC FOOD

AARON THIER

Aaron Thier is the author of three novels, *The Ghost Apple*, *Mr. Eternity*, and *The World Is a Narrow Bridge*. He was a columnist for *Lucky Peach* and a contributor to *The Nation*, and in 2016 he received a Literature Fellowship from the National Endowment for the Arts. He lives in western Massachusetts.

The first time I experienced alcohol withdrawal was also the night a housemate of mine prepared a meal that consisted entirely of alcoholic foods. There was a ham mousse and a parsnip foam, both of which were mostly vodka, and they were raw, so the alcohol wouldn't burn off. I'd been joking about alcoholic food for months, but I was too nauseated to eat anything, alcoholic or not. Something was wrong with me. I'd had a lot to drink the night before, and I'd been hungover that morning, but around that time my hangovers always had a jittery edge. That night, suddenly, I felt half-crazed with anxiety. I went home and tried to sleep, but I couldn't calm down. I saw faces in the darkness. I felt an exquisite and overwhelming dread, as if I were about to be eaten alive. For some reason the theme from *High Noon* was banging around in my head. It didn't occur to me until later that this was withdrawal, because I had no desire for alcohol, it had only been sixteen hours since my last drink, and I hadn't been drinking steadily in any case. I only drank on the weekends, and only at night. I thought I was having a psychotic break. I was a senior in college.

Soon I started taking other

drugs. White pills, green pills, blue pills. Whatever I could find or buy or steal or convince a doctor to prescribe. At the same time it got harder to enjoy food, not just because opioids made me sick and benzodiazepines gave me heartburn, but because it seemed disingenuous to eat good things at a time when I wasn't bothering at all about what I put into my body. I assembled strange impoverished meals, like a single hard-boiled egg and a piece of carrot, or some peanut butter on a hunk of bread. Often I didn't eat at all.

I'd been someone who cared about food. I grew up in western Massachusetts, and my friend's dad raised the beef and pork we ate. My mom was on the board of our co-op. We got our vegetables from a local organic farm long before anyone knew what a CSA was. Mom would sneak celeriac into the roasted potatoes, and I ate lots of beets, and I knew that rhubarb leaves were poisonous and cucumbers were a type of melon. I remember getting into trouble for putting a bumper sticker on the back door when I was very small. It said: "Think Sustainable, Eat Locally Grown."

All of this meant that as things got worse for me and I began to think less and less about what I ate, I also began to lose an important connection to the life I understood to be my own. I felt the sadness and strangeness of this loss and sometimes I struggled against it. I'd get sober for a little while and make a point of going to farmers markets and making food I liked, a casserole or a stew, roast potatoes, beets, the food I'd eaten as a kid. One fall I was taking a break from drinking and I helped out on a farm where a friend of mine was working. At lunch we'd eat whatever we'd been harvesting and packing in the morning, big simple farm salads with boiled potatoes, carrots, sweet onions, eggs, cheese, greens, cured meat. I have never enjoyed food so much. But this lasted only a few months, and soon I was drinking and taking pills again, and I was too hungover to leave the house in the morning. I'd lie around watching movies I'd already seen and eating frozen pizza. It made me unhappy to think that anyone else might think that I was eating the pizza because I enjoyed it. I refused to turn the heat on until November and wore a coat indoors.

A few years later, I broke my own hand so that I could get Percocet. I was high for a month and all I ate were caramels that my uncle and cousin made. One fall, when I was working in a research lab, I forgot my lunch and decided to replace the calories by drinking molecular-biology-grade ethanol. I didn't regret decisions like these. I didn't care at all. Because of the drugs, but not only because of the drugs, everything seemed muted and subdued. Only when I was in withdrawal did I feel the dread.

That year, I celebrated Thanksgiving by taking an overdose of barbiturates. This happened at my parents' house, and it is a kind of blessing that I remember almost none of it, but I do remember the meal I enjoyed at the hospital: it was a charcoal smoothie in a big polystyrene cup.

And then one April day, while I was in graduate school in north Florida, I woke up and my feet were swollen. I sat there for a long time looking at them. The visual effect was interesting and unnerving. I'd been up most of the night drinking, and I had no idea what was happening or where I'd been.

I went down to the courtyard and tried to read John Berryman poems in the hot sun. My vision was blurry and I could hardly make out the words, which was just as well. Suddenly, looking at my feet again, I felt a sweet exhaustion settle over me. There was no shame or anger or

> "I'd eat fifteen pancakes for breakfast. I'd eat four or five pints of strawberries. An entire watermelon. Blueberries from the yard, blackcaps in the woods. A whole pie."
>
> —Aaron Thier

fear, all of which came later. There was only this clean wrinkled feeling of a rag that had been washed and wrung out. That was the last time I was hungover.

I spoke to my mom that afternoon. I felt calm, but I must have said something alarming, because she immediately sent me a plane ticket and I went home the next morning. It was rainy and cool in Massachusetts. I spent the first few weeks splitting firewood and sweating through a painful and terrifying period of benzodiazepine withdrawal. Then I started to feel better, and then much better, and by midsummer I was visiting the farm and exercising and hiking and watching the World Cup. But I was also eating enormous quantities of food, not as a replacement for drugs, or as a matter of neurotic compulsion, but as a way of enjoying a feeling of good health that I hadn't known for many years. My mom would make a batch of oatmeal cookies and I'd eat them in one sitting. I'd eat fifteen pancakes for breakfast. I'd eat four or five pints of strawberries. An entire watermelon. Blueberries from the yard, blackcaps in the woods. A whole pie. Mom and Dad would cook and I would eat, and then I would charge around and burn it all off. It was the food I'd had as a kid, and I felt that I was picking up a thread I'd abandoned years before. I felt like I was turning back into the sober and serious-minded person I'd been at eight years old.

When I was well enough, I went back to Florida. My mom gave me a binder full of recipes to take with me. Simple things, like Indian cabbage, shortbread, and roast chicken. The first thing I did when I got back was flush all the drugs down the toilet, but the second thing I did was try to make oatmeal cookies. I ended up with a single giant rectangular cookie that I couldn't get off the sheet. In the past, this might have struck me as a miserable and pathetic thing, but I just chipped it into a big bowl and ate it with a spoon. Three weeks later, still shaky and a little crazed, but more myself every day, I met my wife.

Oatmeal Cookies

¾ cup butter, softened
1 cup dark brown sugar
½ cup granulated sugar
1 egg
1 teaspoon vanilla

¼ cup water
3 cups rolled oats
½ teaspoon baking soda
1 teaspoon salt
1 cup flour

To make actual cookies, cream butter and sugar, then add the egg and vanilla, then add everything else. Bake at 350°F for 12 to 15 minutes. It's possible an ungreased cookie sheet would work, but parchment paper is always a good bet. The trick to making a single hard sheet of oat dessert is to warm the butter up too much at the beginning, so it leaks out while the cookies bake. Then they'll stick and dry out and you can use a butter knife to chip them off.

BAKE YOUR FEAR

RAKESH SATYAL

Rakesh Satyal is the author of the novels *Blue Boy* and *No One Can Pronounce My Name*. *Blue Boy* won a Lambda Literary Award and the Prose/Poetry Award from the Association of Asian American Studies and was a finalist for a Publishing Triangle Award. Satyal was a 2010 Fellow in Fiction courtesy of the New York Foundation for the Arts. His writing has appeared in *New York* magazine, *Vulture*, *Out* magazine, *The Awl*, and *them*. He has taught in the publishing program at New York University, has sat on the advisory committee for the annual PEN World Voices Festival, and serves on the board of Lambda Literary. He is currently a senior editor at Atria Books, a division of Simon & Schuster. He and his husband live in Brooklyn.

For most of my childhood, I had guys who cornered me in the hallways at school or tormented me on the bus rides home; there were the times when someone would rip a book from my hands and throw it across the playground or trip me so that I fell face-first into the dirt underneath the swings. When you are in the throes of bullying, when you are facing the physical terror of it, the menace that could be something as intangible as a glare or something as tangible as a punch, it is not a term but an entire state of fear. This is all the more reason that, once you escape whatever threat has been immediately in front of you, you seek out something over which you have control, materials and tools and processes that you can use to make something beautiful. As a queer person, being creative—exercising the right of creativity, the liberation it could provide, the solace it could generate—was an act of survival on my part. So it's no great surprise that I turned to pie, a literal enclosure of taste, as a means of comfort.

Pie—that quintessential symbol of coziness and culinary Americana, a dish so enticing that being simply left on a windowsill to cool causes it, in caricature, to extend wavy tendrils of scent into the surrounding air and draw neighbors in by their noses. Sadly, although I grew up in decidedly suburban Ohio, we weren't so rural as to have pies cooling on windowsills. My family was Indian; we weren't in the habit of making pies at all. Instead, my mother would either make *barfi*, a traditional Indian confection composed of sweet condensed milk, coconut, and cardamom, or Betty Crocker chocolate cakes from mixes, which my dad brought home from his job at General Mills.

Perhaps because it wasn't a mainstay in my daily life, perhaps because it wasn't informed by my parents' immediate cultural understanding, and perhaps because it *was*

in that rarefied world of American culinary comfort, I turned to pie-making as a coping mechanism. I figured that if I actually made the confections readily associated with those who were tormenting me, I might circumvent the sometimes-brutal circumstances in which I found myself. Why not commit to something so dearly embraced by American culture to see if it would legitimize me more? There were TV mothers who made them so deftly, who seemed so content in their willful production of edible Americana, and I could join their ranks, for I, too, had become adept at taking the things the world could give me and turning them into something more beautiful, more bolstering—or at the very least, something that might make me less disliked.

I remember the first pie that I ever made: apple, of course, but I forgot to remove the peels from the apples themselves, so the filling included the tough red skin. Meanwhile, I had also forgotten to cover the pie's edges with foil for the better part of the baking process, so when it came out of the oven, it resembled the opposite of a solar eclipse image in a science book—a bright center and a burnt corona surrounding it.

There would be better and more refined pies to come. Once I had mastered the art of making a crust—at the age of thirteen—I was free to experiment with whatever I wanted to include within it. All manner of fruits were explored—only fitting for a queer person—and then there was the requisite period in which I made savory things, quiches and tarts and pastries assembled from reconstituted dough.

Doing my homework, I found myself doodling pies on my notebook while I sat at the dining room table, or into my problem sets during particularly tedious lectures in math class. (But not during language arts, when I was too busy devouring the literary discussion to focus on anything else.) Soon enough, I was drawing pies that sprouted wings, or over which a halo of light hovered, or that had musical notes wafting out of them along with their aroma. The scariness of the world around

me meant that I had to contain my ostentation within myself, but I *could* unfetter it on the page, as deftly as my hands stirred together blueberries and sugar and cinnamon for a filling.

This out-of-the-box thinking (or out-of-the-pie-plate thinking) led me to try out intricate shapes that I added to my crusts. That's right: this queen knows how to accessorize her pastries, *mmmk?* I'd roll dough into little discs that I'd wrap around each other to create roses and other shapes, and I'd bake them separately and then add them to the top of my pies. This was basically my version of waving a Pride flag before I could officially come out. (Years later, I still mention this to my parents: "You really didn't know when I made blueberry pies with *floral arrangements* on them?")

People often deride cooking as a chore or an unnecessarily taxing undertaking, an activity that exacerbates stress instead of relieving it. Even more people seem to deride baking, in particular—the meticulousness of measurement it stipulates, the sheer number of steps it takes to transform dry and wet ingredients into a cake adorned in icing, a cookie studded with chips, and yes, a pie crisscrossed in sugar-speckled strips. But those of us who love baking love it for the very reason that others shy away from it: the praxis of it, the dexterity of movement and imagination of its construction and the boundaries that can be teased out and pushed. These make it worth the mental exercise and acuity, and then there is the coup de grâce: the finished product itself, physical proof of the thought and careful stewardship that went into it. And, well, it's pretty. (Unless it's mincemeat. That shit looks medieval.)

Since the election, I have basically salted the inside of my pies with my own tears. (Yes, this is pretty much a plot point of the movie *Waitress* and its musical-theater incarnation.) But I continue to find deep comfort in seeing this sweet creation that I've brought into the world, this fruity embodiment of my efforts to soldier forth in the face of adversity. It's become, fittingly, a kind of mantra: *Take your fear. Bake your fear. And make your fear go away.*

Rakesh's Florid Blueberry Pie

FOR THE CRUST

2 cups all-purpose white
   flour
⅛ teaspoon salt
⅔ cup shortening

7 to 10 tablespoons water
⅛ teaspoon sugar
1 egg beaten with 1 tablespoon
   water

FOR THE FILLING

1 cup sugar
1 tablespoon flour
1 tablespoon cinnamon
1 teaspoon nutmeg
3 to 4 cups blueberries,
   washed
1 teaspoon lemon zest

1 teaspoon orange zest
1 tablespoon freshly squeezed
   lemon juice
1 tablespoon human tears
2 tablespoons butter, cut into
   pieces

Preheat oven to 425°F. In a mixing bowl, mix flour and salt for the crust. Add shortening and cut into the flour-salt mixture until the result is grainy. Add water 1 tablespoon at a time and stir; you want the dough to be soft but not too sticky. Once finished, halve the dough but make one half slightly larger than the other. Set the larger half aside. Roll the smaller half out into a circle and then place in pie plate, shaving off any excess dough. Keep excess dough for later.

In another mixing bowl, combine dry ingredients for the filling. Fold blueberries into the mixture, coating them. Add in the lemon and orange zests and mix well. Scoop into pie plate, then dot with lemon juice and human tears and cut pieces of butter.

Take the other half of dough and roll it out. Sprinkle one end of it with the sugar and roll it once more. Cover the pie plate with the sugared top up, trimming off excess dough once more and saving it. To seal, either pinch around the pie plate using a thumb and forefinger or take a fork and press grooves all around the edge. Carve two to four slits into the center of the crust to allow steam to escape while cooking. Baste the crust with the beaten egg and water (egg wash); save a small amount for the floral decorations to come. Cover the edges of the crust with tin foil to prevent burning while baking.

Bake in oven for 35 to 45 minutes; remove foil about half an hour into the baking. While the pie is baking, take the extra dough and roll bits of it into pea-sized balls. Take each ball and press it flat with your thumb. Then, roll one of the circles so that it forms a cone-like shape. Press more discs of dough onto it, fastening them at the bottom to create a rose-like ornament. Make however many you want or use the extra dough to make leaves. Brush with the remaining egg wash. Once the pie is done baking and has been removed from the oven, bake the shapes on a baking sheet for about 5 to 10 minutes, until the very tips begin to brown.

Let the pie cool for 15 to 20 minutes, and once they're done baking, allow the flowers and leaves about 5 minutes to cool. Decorate the pie with the flowers and leaves and serve.

THE SWEET POTATO YEAR

JESSICA SOFFER

Jessica Soffer's work has appeared in *Granta*, *The New York Times*, *Martha Stewart Living*, *Real Simple*, *Redbook*, *Saveur*, *The Wall Street Journal*, and *Vogue* and on NPR's *Selected Shorts*. Her bestselling novel, *Tomorrow There Will Be Apricots*, was published in twelve countries. She lives in Sag Harbor, New York, and hosts retreats at five-star inns that focus on writing through the lens of food.

I was raised with an understanding of food as the ultimate remedy. My father was an Iraqi Jew and his mother was a healer in Baghdad. She believed in eating for both nourishment and well-being. Growing up, we drank lemon water and ate quinoa and kale. We had bright and bitter herbs in spring and warming ones in winter. When I was sick: turmeric/ginger/Manuka honey. When I was sad: yellow and orange produce for happiness.

I always knew I wanted to write about this way of eating, and in my first book, I did. Putting good food into the work also meant putting good food into my belly, so during the years of writing it, I ate well. There was constant recipe testing: cardamom cookies, long-stewed soups, okra and eggplant, crumbles and quiches, cocktails and mocktails, and a lot of apricots, dried and pickled and roasted and jammed.

Then, the next book happened. Probably there is a better way to describe it.

But for a year, all I did was

describe. I wrote as if in a fever, with my head down, without coming up for air. I wrote and wrote and wrote. The writing demanded all the everything from me. I had no idea which way was up, where my keys, my socks, my head were. I had conversations, taught, drove. I did laundry and dishes, but barely.

I cooked and ate, but barely, too.

Food mattered less. For the writing, for life.

And though, as I wrote, I was always hungry, I didn't stop. I didn't want to lose momentum. I didn't want to sacrifice mental energy or space on meal planning or prepping or trips to the store or make anything that required complicated knife-work or more than one vessel to clean. For that year, food was fuel. I inhaled pints of raspberries, rice cakes, and avocados without so much as looking away from the computer screen. I ate because I had to. I wrote because I had to. I hunkered down. I listened

"I wrote as if in a fever, with my head down, without coming up for air."

— Jessica Soffer

to instrumental music and tried my damnedest to give the writing a womb in which to grow: protected and meditative and temperate. I avoided fast movements, loud noises, and real cooking.

In the end, I finished a draft. The time it took to do so was the most heartening, empowering, creative period of my life. I fell down the rabbit hole. I gave it my heart and soul. I forgot everything else . . . or I mostly forgot.

Sometimes, I'd think of my father, the mindful eater, and his mother, the healer. I'd remember: Yellow and orange produce for happiness. Stepping away from the computer. Breathing deep, eating well: for the writing, for the heart. And then, I'd take out the steamer, a few simple, vibrant ingredients, and a sharp knife. I'd make this, again and again and again so I could feel good and then, get back to the writing. Again and again and again.

Steamed Japanese Sweet Potato Bowl

sauce: tamari, toasted
   sesame oil, white miso,
   rice vinegar, and honey,
   all shook up in a jar
1 Japanese sweet potato
   (but you can use the
   traditional variety if
   you prefer something
   sweeter and less dense),
   steamed

1 whole zucchini, cut into rounds
   and roasted until chip-like at
   400°F
2 spoonfuls cashew butter
½ cup plain, tart yogurt
sometimes, quarter of an avocado,
   chopped and sprinkled with salt
sprinkle of chopped scallions
sprinkle of chopped, roasted cashews
black sesame seeds

In a deep, cozy bowl, add sauce. On top, and to the side, the steamed sweet potato, mashed up a bit. Next to it, zucchini. Next to that, cashew butter. Then, yogurt. Then, avocado, if you like. And around and around we go. Then, top off everything with scallions, cashews, black sesames. Eat when the potato is hot and everything else is room temperature. And enjoy!

THE DINNER

DARIN STRAUSS

Darin Strauss is the author of the bestselling novels *Chang & Eng*, *The Real McCoy*, *More Than It Hurts You*, the award-winning memoir *Half a Life*, and a bestselling comic-book series, *Olivia Twist*. The recipient of a Guggenheim Fellowship, a National Book Critics Circle Award, and an American Library award, Strauss has been translated into fourteen languages and published in nineteen countries. His next novel, *The Queen of Tuesday*, is due out in 2020, along with a graphic novel based on the Olivia Twist series. Strauss has collaborated on screenplays with Gary Oldman and Julie Taymor, and is the Clinical Professor of fiction in the NYU Graduate Writing Program.

One time, years ago, I freeze-framed the ex-pitcher Mariano Rivera in his motion—his elbow a tight corner straight above his head, the back arched like a sail in his white uniform—and I saw something, an almost Guinness Bookish anomaly. Mid-toss, his body was all drawing-board angles. The great athletes look *different*. They look different even doing the mundane—tossing a ball, skimming across the boxing ring, pulling a bat from the rack and practice-swinging. YouTube old Michael Jordan: see the poise and space-alien rigor he shows just dribbling up the court. Watch Steph Curry's wrists.

My wife Susannah is like that with motherhood.

Watch her tend to Beau's cut knee; or, if our other son, Shepherd, forgets his homework, see her comfort and cajole. Or, just see how much effort she puts into the meals she cooks every night. Susannah is the author of *The Other Side of Impossible*, which is about people faced with difficult health conditions who have exhausted medicine's answers. Often these people find help in food—the science of the kitchen, the medicine of the everyday. And so my wife makes sure our family eats a multitude of the right vegetables and fruits and generally salubrious, organic food. Every single day.

How does one compete with this Pete Sampras of Parenthood? One doesn't—or only does rarely.

More about those kids: My sons are identical twins. And they are nearly identical, looks-wise. Except Beau has short hair, and Shepherd's has turned his head, at ten, into a close approximation of Jim Morrison's. As *people* they're quite different, and quite wonderful. I'll tell you two representative stories about them.

One hot summer day, I took Beau to the aquarium. We watched a big sea lion who'd flippered its way out of the water and was sunning itself on the concrete. A creature from a wetter world. Its wet and thick skin looked so shiny—it seemed almost like a moving brown liquid. Lots of people watched the sea lion. And when the trainer poked it, the animal rolled over into the pool with a bellyfloppy whomp. Everybody laughed. Or, almost everybody did. I did. Beau didn't, though. He was about six, or maybe five. The sea lion stayed under water for a long time. And when its little brown face finally peered out of the water, he smiled. "Oh, great," he said. "He's not hurt." And then he laughed, at last. "I just wanted to make sure he wasn't hurt. It made me sad that everyone was laughing at him."

Shepherd's story comes from this past winter. He was ten, and we had arrived at the hill for sledding in Brooklyn's Prospect Park. Mittens, shouts. Everyone there had either a round, sittable bowl or a plastic toboggan sled. Only Shepherd had a very strange contrivance: a Razor Kick Scooter, with little plastic skis over the wheels. Kids looked at him, as we shlumped in our boots to the hill.

"Wow," ten-year-old Shepherd said. "My sled is fairly exotic." His smile turned all the way up, something warm in that winter snow. "It's like I brought a giraffe to a dog park."

I can only recall one time when my wife didn't achieve Greatest of All Time status for her mothering. When Shepherd was three years old, he was diagnosed with juvenile rheumatoid arthritis. It came on suddenly, and hit hard. Here's how Susannah described it: "It sounded more odd than alarming at first, but over the next few weeks, we watched Shepherd spend more and more time on the couch. His stiff-legged walk became more pronounced, though he claimed that he was just walking like a penguin. Then he started having trouble getting out of bed."

This flattened my wife and me. But she *really* lost it: Within a few days, she lost her purse, her suitcase, and got into a car accident. I had to take charge, and that included preparing meals.

One night I made this dinner: cod with a mustard garlic sauce; kale chips; sweet potatoes; and a salad with homemade dressing. It tasted familiar, and the kids loved it. ("Dad, pretty good," Beau said. "Yes," said Shepherd, who adores his mother, "almost as good as Mom's.") These dishes became my go-to. And although my wife usually commands the kitchen, I still make it on occasion to delight my kids and give my wife a break.

I should add that Shepherd ended up fine. That's how my wife came up with the idea for her book. *We* had exhausted medicine, or thought we had. Shepherd wasn't responding to Methotrexate, the "gold standard," as our doctor kept telling us. But Susannah's sister's sister-in-law had a friend—how lucky we were to find this person—who told us her son had juvenile rheumatoid arthritis and got better on a gluten- and dairy-free diet. We tried it—in conjunction with the Methotrexate—very skeptically. But what could it hurt to try, as long as we kept the medicine going? In six weeks, he was better. When we took him of the medicine—slowly, slowly, in conjunction with our doctor—Shepherd was cured.

I don't ever feel like a parent on the same plane as my wife, let alone father of the year or anything. But recently when Susannah was away, speaking about her book, I cooked this meal again for the boys and me. We ate and laughed and relished every bite, and then Susannah came back and demoted me again, restoring equilibrium.

Cod Fillets

1 teaspoon Dijon mustard
1 clove pressed garlic
½ cup mayonnaise
  (preferably homemade)
3 cod fillets (total of
  1 ½ lbs. or 675 g)

½ lemon, juiced
1 teaspoon salt
1 teaspoon black pepper
sprinkle of herbs de Provence

Preheat oven to 350°F.

Mix mustard, garlic, and mayonnaise in a bowl.

Rinse cod fillets under water and pat dry.

Put aluminum foil on cooking pans, then place fillets on the pans.

Coat the fillets with the mustard, garlic, and mayonnaise mixture.

Drizzle lemon juice over the fillets.

Sprinkle the salt, pepper, and herbs on the fillets.

Cook for 18 minutes. The cod is done when it flakes easily when chopped with a fork.

Kale Chips

2 bunches kale

2 tablespoons extra-
virgin olive oil

½ teaspoon salt

Preheat the oven to 375°F.

Rinse kale and pat dry thoroughly.

Pull the leaves from the ribs.

Put leaves on a baking sheet, with aluminum foil. Kale does not need to be in a single layer; it will shrink.

Spread olive oil and sprinkle salt on the kale.

Cook till slightly browned, 15 to 20 minutes.

Sweet Potatoes

3 medium sweet
potatoes, unpeeled

3 tablespoons olive oil

½ teaspoon salt

Heat oven to 375°F.

Slice sweet potatoes into tons of circles.

Place on a baking sheet lined with foil.

Sprinkle with salt.

Bake about 20 minutes.

Homemade Salad Dressing

1 ⅔ cup olive oil
⅓ cup red wine vinegar
1 teaspoon Dijon mustard

1 clove garlic
pinch of salt
¼ teaspoon ground black pepper

Mix the olive oil and the vinegar together.

Add the mustard.

Press the garlic into the dressing.

Stir.

Add pepper and salt to taste.

MINUTE RICE AND OTHER MIRACLES

AMITAVA KUMAR

Amitava Kumar is a writer and journalist. He was born in Ara, and grew up in the nearby town of Patna, famous for its corruption, crushing poverty, and delicious mangoes. Kumar is the author of several books of nonfiction and two novels. He was awarded a Guggenheim Fellowship for nonfiction and lives in Poughkeepsie, in upstate New York, where he is Helen D. Lockwood Professor of English at Vassar College.

There are many discoveries an immigrant makes during his or her first days in a new country, and for me, one of the first was Minute Rice.

I arrived from India in 1986. My roommate was also Indian, from the same town in Bihar; he and I had gone to university together in Delhi. We had almost no experience with cooking. All through my childhood and youth in India, I had seen rice being made for nearly every meal. Rice would be boiled in a pot for a long time and then, with the lid only partially covering the top, the water would be drained out. There was a name in Hindi for this milky liquid: *marh*. In the village where my grandmother lived, *marh* was allowed to cool in a deep tray and then offered to cattle. But here, in America, in a red-and-white box, there was something called Minute Rice. No water to be drained, and the rice ready in a near-instant. It wasn't just a revelation—it seemed more like a miracle.

But what to eat with the rice?

About a decade earlier, my roommate and I had been members of a scout troop in our hometown, Patna. We learned to light a fire in the woods, blowing at smoky twigs while our eyes watered, a skill we didn't seem to need here in the U.S. We also learned a few basic cooking skills. Did we recall our experience with cooking? We remembered that we needed oil in the cooking pan, but everything else was a blur, barely visible through the wood-smoke of time.

I had clearer recall of what I had seen at my grandmother's house. The kitchen was actually a hut separate from the house; the tree trunk that held up the roof was worn smooth, and sooty cobwebs hung overhead. My grandmother, a religious vegetarian, didn't permit the cooking of meat in the kitchen. As soon as we arrived at the house, a farmhand would be sent off to find a couple of chickens. The cook would busy himself arranging a few bricks on the ground outside the kitchen: he would slap wet clay on the bricks and fashion a makeshift earthen stove. The cook's young helper, a thin lad with a sacred amulet dangling over his bony chest, would be at work nearby, grinding onion, ginger, garlic over on a flat stone. On a battered aluminum plate next to him, there would be arranged turmeric, red chilies, and cumin seeds, sticks of cinnamon, crushed coriander. Once wood was lit in the stove, the clay dried and hardened in minutes. By this time the farmhand would have returned with the chickens and, having discreetly wrung their necks behind a bush, squatted down on the grass to pluck the birds clean.

Here in America, chicken came wrapped in transparent covering in the refrigerated section of the Price Rite near our apartment. The meat looked clean and attractive, but also intimidating. How were we ever going to succeed at cooking those plump chicken parts? We weren't. We didn't even try. We went instead for Price Rite's thin slices of beef. Neither I nor my roommate had eaten beef in India. But immigration meant we were ready for anything; we had decided that change was good. However, one problem remained: spices. Yet knowledge about the aisle containing ethnic groceries was still months in the future, and we remained focused on what we could find most easily, which was small tins of Durkee's spices—weak, inadequate substitutes for the fresh spices I had seen being prepared in my grandmother's village home. Immigrants are supposed to be determined and inventive, but when it came to cuisine, we weren't. We gave in without a fight. We didn't know any better.

So, Minute Rice and thin slices of beef seasoned with Durkee's spices. And we didn't even think about getting greens. All this is baffling to me now, of course. You might ask how long this went on? Months! A recipe for monotony and dietary idiocy. Ultimately we found more spices, including McCormick's Curry Powder, and before the year's end we had

also switched to long-grain rice that took fifteen minutes to cook, adding frozen peas per a friend's suggestion, and cooking chicken thighs. This routine lasted another year.

Looking back, this seems such an appalling confession of our once-impoverished lives, narrowed by a lack of both imagination and knowledge. Yet we were graduate students, stressed about our classes, and with very little money. These were days long before the internet, and we never thought about "wasting" money on cookbooks. There was a lot of anxiety about nearly everything, and, what must also be said, a lot of consolation easily available in the existence of routine, even if the routine consisted of eating the same, somewhat unappetizing yet still vaguely familiar food.

This is how I remember those first evenings in America: My roommate and I would sit down in front of the television with our curry improvisations and devour the colonial drama, Masterpiece

Theatre's *The Jewel in the Crown*. (When our Hungarian neighbor gave us a black-and-white television set, it showed only one channel, the one for public television, but this was perfect.) Our sense of nostalgia and connection came not just from the flavor of our food but from hearing the badly mangled Indian names and the feeling that the series prompted in our hearts, that we had come from a place of exquisite, if sometimes painful, romance.

During a trip back to India about two years after I had been living in the U.S., my cousin wrote down in my journal a recipe for making chicken with green chilies. This was perhaps my first step toward civilization. A year or two later, another graduate student in my program made photocopies of her favorite recipes from a book by Madhur Jaffrey. Over the years, I have acquired recipe books for Indian dishes, and I cook for family and friends nearly every day. My life is now richer, of course, but I have a further confession to make. I use recipes as broadly directional, not as

precise steps to follow to perfection. Proceeding simply by tasting and then improvising, sticking close to a recipe the way a traveler might keep a river in sight while walking in one direction, I arrive at that remote station called dinner. And yet I do have one recipe to share.

A few years ago, an esteemed writer was coming to the town where I now live, Poughkeepsie, New York, and he wanted a restaurant recommendation. I sent him a name but regretted I wasn't going to be around; if I were, I'd have grilled some shrimp for him, Indian-style. No worries, he wrote back, but do send me a recipe.

This is what you must know about this writer. I have never met him but admire him immensely for his sentences. For their stab of taste. They surprise you with their wit, and they're always done just right. If you knew who I was talking about you'd read my recipe and think I was trying to sound casual like him, unaffected, but I so wish I also had his precision. This is the recipe that I composed for him.

Indian-Style Shrimp (with Gin)

1 pound shrimp
yogurt
1 teaspoon turmeric
1 teaspoon cumin
1 teaspoon coriander
½ teaspoon salt
chili powder or chili oil
cilantro (scallion will do)

1 heaping tablespoon ginger-garlic mix from the local Indian/Pak store
2 cloves fresh garlic, minced
fresh ginger, minced
Patak's Vindaloo Curry Paste
Bombay Sapphire gin
tonic water
fresh lemon and pepper for serving

The night before, marinate. Coat a pound of shrimp in yogurt and sprinkle a teaspoon each of turmeric, cumin, and coriander. A little less of salt, I think. Also a bit of chili powder, or better still, chili oil. If there's scallion around, put that in. Or cilantro, which is more authentic. But here's the important part: At the local Indian/Pak store, I get this ginger-garlic mix and add a heaping tablespoon. Now, using this bottled mix leads to a lot of guilt, so I also mince a couple of cloves of fresh garlic and mince an equal amount of ginger to go with it. The fresh stuff doesn't suffice, by the way; I have a near-scientific faith in what comes out of bottles. Which brings us to the final ingredient, even if it's only a spoon or two, and that is the dark matter that comes out of the bottle, again easily available at most stores, Patak's Vindaloo Curry Paste. This paste gives, among other things, the gift of color.

The next afternoon or evening, when you're ready to cook, first pour yourself some gin and tonic. That must always be the first step.

An hour before you start, take the shrimp out of the refrigerator and allow it to return to room temperature. Heat a grill to around 300°F or maybe less if the grill is small. I use these metal skewers I picked up at Stop & Shop; just baste the skewers and the shrimp with olive oil. They take about five minutes per side. I don't let anything other than the tail get singed. Serve it after sprinkling fresh lemon and pepper.

This dish should always be washed down with gin and tonic. For somewhat specious reasons, I only drink Bombay Sapphire.

NO ALZHEIMER'S
IN INDIA

ANTOINE WILSON

Antoine Wilson is the author of the novels *Panorama City* and *The Interloper*. His work has appeared in *The Paris Review*, *StoryQuarterly*, and *Best New American Voices*, among other publications, and he is a contributing editor of the literary magazine *A Public Space*.

When my father died, his third and final wife's family took care of the funeral arrangements. He was eighty-one years old and had been married to my stout Filipina stepmother for maybe eighteen months. They'd lived together in a forgotten corner of Los Angeles, behind a security gate upon which warnings were posted that emergency services couldn't access the home. Through the gate, one could see his favorite car, a 1980s Jaguar XJS which constantly smelled of gasoline, deliquescing into the knee-high grass.

My house was less than ten miles away, but I saw him rarely, usually when he ended up in the hospital with a bout of pancreatitis. I had no sense of how he and my stepmother spent their hours together, other than their managing the ongoing drama which was her import-export company. They were always on the verge of making a very big deal: a boatload of carrageenan, metric tons of gold, shipping containers of concrete headed to Pakistan. The deal inevitably fell through at the last minute, and then another would appear on the horizon. It had all the hallmarks of a scam, but no money ever changed hands.

My father had been a respected surgeon in his day. Once the head of the Quebec Orthopaedic Association, he had practiced in Central California, Southern California, and Saudi Arabia, with stints in Peshawar, Yellowknife, and Fort Leonard Wood: a life of adventure, but also of diminishing returns. Three boys with the first wife in Ottawa, three boys with the French Canadian wife in Montreal, then a move to California. Later: a second divorce, a girlfriend in Canada, a son of questionable parentage, a Filipina girlfriend in Los Angeles.

The memorial ceremony that my stepmother organized featured a bizarre PowerPoint slide show, mostly pictures from my father's eighty-first birthday visit to the Philippines, with primer-like captions ("Bill liked to have fun") and a maudlin soundtrack ("I Will Remember You"). Afterward we listened to a eulogy delivered by a priest who must have been fresh out of seminary: he strained for emotion and marched around as if

the room were twice as large as it was. When the time came for remembrances, about a dozen friends and neighbors got up to speak, all from his life with the third wife. Some admitted to not knowing my father that well.

We, various members of his first two families, watched the whole thing in a state of shock. Finally, ever the responsible one, I made my way to the podium, doing what I could to cut through the extreme awkwardness of the moment. I started with: "My father led many lives . . ."

What else did I say? I don't remember. But I remember what I didn't say. That behind his every adventure was an urge to escape. That his phenomenal intelligence didn't extend to the emotional realm. That he kept trying to get it right, even after he had gotten it right. That the people who had put together this memorial, who loved him and respected him in his later years, had no idea what had come before, the joys and the heartbreak, the triumphs and the wreckage.

Like so many things in his life,

my father's relationship to food was idiosyncratic. His priorities oscillated between sustenance and health. Growing up in the wake of the Great Depression, he was reluctant to spend too much on food. He would regularly pick through bags of wilted lettuce looking for still-edible leaves. The glove box of his car invariably housed a browning banana. He was no gourmet. He'd take a dinner my mother had made—steak, potatoes, salad—and toss it all together on his plate, drowning everything in Worcestershire sauce before eating it.

With his medical background, my father was occasionally drawn to health food, or what fit his idea of health. Left to his own devices, he'd prepare things like wheat germ on wheat toast or air-popped popcorn sprinkled with potassium salt, the health benefits of which were probably mitigated by the accompanying vodka–chocolate milk cocktail. At breakfast once, while the rest of us were passing the maple syrup, he pulled out a small plastic container and unscrewed the lid. He shook it over his French toast, releasing a cloud of bright yellow dust. Turmeric. I asked him what he was doing. "There's no Alzheimer's in India," he explained, taking a big yellow bite, smiling like a madman.

As it turns out, he wasn't so far off the mark. Years later, I discovered that the turmeric-coated toast that had horrified everyone at the breakfast table is in fact akin to Bombay toast, a sometimes-spicy, sometimes-sweet Indian breakfast specialty. In many ways, it's the perfect dish for my father: it's inexpensive, easy to prepare, and you can rescue stale bread on its way to the trash. Plus the dish has bona fide health benefits, turmeric being a natural antiseptic and anti-inflammatory. It's portable, edible in the car on the way to work. And, when made properly, it's delicious.

Looking back at my father's memorial service, I remember a series of awkward, strained moments, followed by a banquet of sad, generic half sandwiches. If it had been my choice, though, I'd have covered those tables with plates of my father's turmeric-coated toast, the unexpected color and flavor filling the drab reception hall with the bright memory of his complicated, contradictory spirit, reminding us exactly who it was we had lost.

No Alzheimer's Turmeric Toast

2 eggs
½ teaspoon vanilla extract
1 tablespoon milk
1 teaspoon sugar
1 teaspoon turmeric
    powder
½ tablespoon cinnamon powder
1 pinch black pepper
1 pinch salt
thick bread, 4 slices
1 tablespoon olive oil, butter, or
    ghee

In a bowl, beat together the eggs, vanilla, milk, sugar, turmeric, and cinnamon. Add a pinch of black pepper and a pinch of salt.

Soak slices of bread in the egg mixture until saturated.

Heat a bit of the olive oil or butter (or both) in a pan.

Fry each slice over medium heat, until brown.

Top with powdered sugar, fruit, and/or maple syrup.

Alternately, for savory toast, omit the sugar and cinnamon and add more black pepper to taste. Mix in a scallion, chopped thinly. Top with hot sauce of choice.

ONE SIP AT A TIME

ALISSA NUTTING

Alissa Nutting is an assistant professor of English and writer in residence at Grinnell College. She is author of the novels *Made for Love* and *Tampa*, as well as the story collection *Unclean Jobs for Women and Girls*.

One December, about two weeks before Christmas, my then-husband of twelve years moved out. Our daughter was one and a half.

Inside me, a very odd, manic, uncomfortable energy powered on. It felt like an engine, and I had no way of turning it off. I couldn't sleep at all unless I took prescription medication. I had horrible pain in my back muscles. I tried to describe the feeling to a doctor, and then a chiropractor, and then an acupuncturist.

"It's like two hundred babies are all punching me at once, all over my back with tiny fists," I told them. This alarmed the chiropractor and

acupuncturist. They did what they could, though nothing helped. The doctor just challenged my simile. "Babies really can't punch that hard," she pointed out.

I tried everything to feel less awful. I spent money I should've been giving to my divorce lawyer on crystals and Reiki. The Reiki practitioner often made psychic guesses about my life based on the energy she was picking up, and all her guesses were incorrect. But I'm conflict-averse so I told her everything she was saying was true.

I also couldn't eat. At all. I had zero hunger or craving for food. After a few days, I started to feel faint at work, and I knew I had to do something. But I truly couldn't chew and swallow food. I could drink, though, so on the advice of a nutrition-savvy friend, I started drinking green juice. Formerly a professional snacker, I went from eating junk food round-the-clock to drinking only vegetables.

Weight melted off me. Too much. Friends grew concerned. People tried to feed me solid food hourly. "Just eat!" they'd say. "Just do it!" But I couldn't, and I had no explanation as to why.

"Do you feel like if you eat you're feeding him?" one friend asked. "That eating would be like giving your ex power?"

I loved the elegant complexity of this theory. I wanted my starvation to be fueled by this reasoning. I tried convincing myself that it was. I could picture the more sophisticated version of myself in a parallel universe who might have this psychology. Me but with excellent posture. Me but following a skincare regimen. Me but wearing silk caftans to bed and not letting trash pile up on the floor of my car.

My truth was basic and involved no willpower: I just had no appetite. Imagine tripping on store-brand cough syrup twenty-four hours a day, except without the benefits of hallucinatory visuals or fruit flavoring. I felt wired and on edge and exceptionally paranoid. Eating seemed impossible.

Now that three years have passed, I'm sturdy enough to look back at my behavior with a critical eye and question this. Did I subconsciously go on a hunger strike to try to get my ex's attention? Was it a last-ditch effort to manipulate or guilt him into staying? To worry him to the point that he'd break down and admit he actually still cared about me? (Side note: he sure didn't do this.) I guess it's possible. But it felt like something that was controlling me, not the other way around.

After about a week of drinking the juice, I began to feel like a plant. In moments of panic, it was actually a little fun to pretend this. *You're growing*, I told myself. *You got chopped down but you're growing back.* I carried a bottle of green juice wherever I went, and anytime I found myself hungry or thirsty or dizzy or scared or confused or annoyed or unsure, I'd take a sip.

People have a lot of questions for you when you're going through a sad and painful event like divorce. When I didn't want to answer them, I'd shrug and take a sip of juice.

One of the only social events I'd engaged in prior to the divorce was a bar night once a week where several local authors got together and drank. I knew I was in no condition for alcohol. In the past I never let that detail hinder me, but this time I did. I found this fascinating even in the moment; it will always fascinate me because I love drinking. I was taking care of a very young child, though, and during this time I knew that one beer would lead to twenty. So every week I took the thermos of green juice to the bar. When I felt tempted, the green juice was there as a reminder: I had plenty left to lose, and I didn't want to lose it.

It took a few months, but my appetite did gradually come back. During my green-juice-only period, I was sure I'd be drinking and craving it for the rest of my life. The more food I ate, the more I realized: so many things taste even better. I phased it out as abruptly as I'd started it.

But it kept me alive on days I didn't feel sure I could make it to the next minute. Every now and again, I'll make a batch as a kind of victory lap. When living felt impossible, I got through it one sip at a time.

Green Juice

1 ½ cups water
2 cups kale
2 green apples, cored
½ cup parsley leaves
1 medium cucumber, quartered

2 celery stalks, roughly
  chopped
1 (1-inch) piece of ginger,
  peeled
2 tablespoons lemon juice

Add all ingredients to your blender and blend it until it's liquefied.

Homecoming

DARK LEAVES AND WARM MILK

MIRA JACOB

Mira Jacob is the author of the critically acclaimed novel *The Sleepwalker's Guide to Dancing* and the graphic memoir *Good Talk*. Her recent work has appeared in *The New York Times*, the *Virginia Quarterly Review*, *Vogue*, and *Glamour*, among others. She lives, draws, and writes in Brooklyn with her husband and son.

Something terrible has happened. It could be the boys in fourth grade calling you a monkey, it could be your high school best friend going after another of your exes, it could be not getting pregnant despite months of trying and coming from a continent of seemingly endlessly fertile women. Your face is a cracked plate.

"Let's make tea," your mother will say, and you will nod because this is how all of your life's disasters have tasted, like dark leaves and warm milk.

She will put the water on and you will move like bandits robbing your own kitchen. Two minutes later, on the counter: the box of Red Label, the milk jug, ginger, mint leaves, cloves, cardamom, the cinnamon bark from Ammachy's tree—the one that started growing on farmland and now sits right in the middle of a small town in Kerala, as unfazed by modernity as your grandmother herself. ("I understand American problems," she once wrote you in the nineties, her tiny script faint against the blue airmail pages. "I watch the Oprah every day.")

"We are a cliché," you say as you microplane the ginger and your mother raises her eyebrows. "Indians making chai."

"I always just mince the ginger," she says.

You throw the spices into the water and go into the pantry to hunt down Salt & Pepper potato chips because tea without a savory is as comforting as a mattress without sheets. You pull your favorite mugs from a large and mismatched collection. When the water boils, you switch it off, first adding the tea, then the milk.

"I always warm the milk separately," your mother says.

Two minutes later, you strain it all into the pot and add sugar because your mother disapproves of people adding their own sugar individually. ("Joyless," she will say, and she will be right.)

When it is all ready, you will sit at the kitchen table and drink from tiny terracotta mugs. You will not tell your mother about being called a monkey. You will not tell her about the ex-best friend. You will not tell her about being worried you waited too long to try to have kids because she will say you probably did because the truth is, your mother is terrible at hearing your hurts. She spews platitudes, she shrugs her shoulders, she pinpoints what you might have done better. Always, though, the pain in her eyes is bright, as though she has directly imbibed whatever misery you feel at a much higher intensity, as though she would curl her body around yours to leach out the rest if possible.

It is not possible for your mother to take your disasters from you, and it's that tiny piece of knowledge that you save yourselves from by sipping slowly, by talking about the neighbor's kids and political scandals and anything else you can think of to fill the silence. When it creeps up again, your mother pats your hand twice.

"Pass the chips," she says, and you do.

Chai

3 cups water

1 cup milk

8 teaspoons loose black
   Red Label tea leaves

1 teaspoon ginger,
   microplaned (heavier
   flavor) or minced (lighter
   flavor)

5 whole green cardamom
   seeds, cracked

5 cloves

1 teaspoon dried mint, or 5
   minced fresh leaves

1 inch cinnamon bark, broken
   into a few pieces

3 tablespoons sugar

Heat water and spices until it comes to a fragrant boil. Turn
down to simmer for one minute. Turn off heat. Add tea and milk.
Let steep for two minutes for lighter tea, longer if you prefer a
slight bitterness. Add sugar to taste and strain to serve.

CLEANSE

ALEXANDER CHEE

Alexander Chee is the author of the novels *Edinburgh* and *The Queen of the Night* and the essay collection *How to Write an Autobiographical Novel*. He is a contributing editor at *The New Republic* and an editor at large at *VQR*. His essays and stories have appeared in *The New York Times Book Review*, *T Magazine*, *Tin House*, *Slate*, *Guernica*, and *Out*, among others. He is an associate professor of English and creative writing at Dartmouth College.

You should do that cleanse, my brother says. We're sitting in a raw foods store, in the alcove they provide for people to eat their extraordinarily priced delicious raw vegan snacks. It's hard for me not to see it all as vegetarianism for rich people, because, well, I am not a rich person, but my brother is now. I feel something like a class obligation lingering for me to pick up on, as I turn the mysterious packages over and read the ingredients: Irish sea moss, Himalayan sea salt, organic figs.

The world, shaken out or down, for a smoothie.

When we were kids, my brother and I would sneak off and get Philly cheesesteak subs with mushrooms and mayo on white bread rolls. Now he's a financier with a mostly vegetarian wife and both have a penchant for raw foods, which is why we've stopped here. And though I was the first in my family to flirt with veganism, back in the 1980s, after Courtney Love announced "Cheese makes you fat," I'm now one of those lapsed vegetarians, trapped in the world of meat by a love of bacon. And, well, cheese (sorry, Courtney!).

I agree to the cleanse, a birthday gift from him, something of a concession—he is worried about my health. I'm not the skinny ex–yoga instructor I once was a decade ago. We first discussed it months before this visit, and I have been taking my time at signing up for it. Mostly because of how a cleanse can put you into a state of rage, as my brother warned, chuckling at some memory—and I do also know this. I also know that once you say the word "cleanse," once you have it somewhere ahead of you in your future, not doing it seems, well, untenable, like leaving your house not just a mess but *dirty*. You start to feel like a sponge someone pulled out of the Gowanus Canal that grew legs. I know this because I've cleansed before—see under "ex–yoga instructor"—and I know too well how the food you eat most of the time is revealed to be not food at all, just hidden sugar, hidden ad-dictions. Sometimes not so hidden. You call it breakfast but it's really "don't think about my job now

thanks" with a side of toast. Take that away and replace it with an aloe shot, and your life comes into view.

Who am I, though, really, if I can't look at my life?

I walk over to the counter with him and we sign me up. Yes, five days, I say to the clerk, as my brother raises an eyebrow. We're brothers, after all. And still a little competitive, even here.

ON THE FIRST DAY OF THE cleanse, I'm a little afraid. I have not gone without a cup of coffee a day since I was sixteen. The one time I tried, in fact, my brother called, and when I mentioned I was on a cleanse, giving up coffee, he said, "Don't do that. Make coffee and call me back."

Coffee is one thing I do drink organic, as much as possible. Who wants a cup of DDT every day? The pesticides they are allowed to use in other countries outside the U.S. are terrifying things. Also the ones we use inside the U.S.

I manage everything except the coffee. I go almost the full day without it. The alcohol is much easier to give up, a relief. It is easy to joke you are an alcoholic only when you are not really an alcoholic.

The plan is organized to stimulate the body's cleansing of itself—aloe shots and green juices in the morning, an entrée at lunch, a salad at dinner, smoothies and juices alternating throughout. Taken as a whole, it's a recipe for a cleaner you. The packages arrive every day in silver lamé boxes set inside safety orange bags, as if delivered from a vegan disco. The smoothies and juices are in thick glass bottles, like the old milk bottles—this vegan disco has also liberated a dairy somewhere, it seems. The entrées are in what we call plastic jewelboxes, though nothing has ever looked less like a jewelbox. These few actual foods are often delicious replicas of the rich foods we give up for this cleanse, but said to be empty of poisons and animal fats and sugars—raw lasagna is one favorite, made with slices of zucchini or squash instead of pasta. Or a "chocolate shake," made with cacao, coconut milk, dates, and that moss—but is the moss Irish, or Himalayan, too, and am I eating

moss now? These are what are delivered on my plan, which is said to be the gentle one.

Dairy and wheat are entirely eliminated. These most common of foods are not common because they are so nourishing—they are common because they are easy to mass-produce.

I spend the first day feeling both pampered and abstemious. But when I enter the store to return the bottles, I feel myself to be in disguise among the rich, vibrantly healthy vegetarians. And on my way home to my Hell's Kitchen apartment, the people in the restaurants lining the streets look monstrous, the food they eat, horrific, food I would have thought of eating just the other day. I feel like I've taken mushrooms.

When I find an article in a friend's Facebook feed about in vitro meat farms being planned, because of the enormous cost to the environment of raising all this meat, it's like discovering I live in the monstrous future I feared as a child, a childhood spent watching science fiction films about the monstrous future. And in my cleanse-induced trance, the in vitro burger looms like the biggest monster of all. The scientists hope it is going to save us from our burger habit, which is just one of the things killing us. Global warming turns out to be a lot like leaving a burger on the stove too long, but a burger the size of Brazil, say, or North America. A burger that burns fields as it grows and then again as it cooks.

I can't take it anymore. I feel broken, weak after one day without coffee, dairy, wheat, meat. I lie down. I see the person I have always been until now, the person I thought I was, like a man in a motorboat, racing across the sea. The sea which is also me.

Who am I?

I get up and make coffee. Because that is who I am.

IN THE BATHROOM, YOUR NEW favorite place during a cleanse, you feel virtuous every time you flush. Goodbye, poison, I think, as I leave. Goodbye.

ON DAY TWO, I FIND MYSELF thinking about the world's population, eating, eating, eating. It's the burger, still on my mind, the in vitro burger to save us all.

The seven billionth kid was born last year, wasn't he? Weren't we going to try to find him, by which I mean, some ridiculous television show? We should consider it. He would be like the democratic opposite of the reborn Tibetan llamas, just an ordinary kid who just happens to be number seven billion. When I do think about him, though, I can feel how Planet Earth is now seven billion people who don't yet seem to all know they need to convince four hundred people who have all of the money and power to change how we are all living so we can survive what will happen to our planet in the next fifty years, and then I want to lie down. But I can't. Because I know those four hundred people think of the seven billion of us as people auditioning to be the survivors who get to flip that burger.

Most times I can't think about it, like many of you, no doubt. But then it comes back, in the little things. This is what I think of when I see cars on this second day, when they roar past my New York apartment window on Tenth Avenue, our communal death turning on the wheels. It is what I think of as I open the jewelbox to take out the day's entrée—the jewelbox is recycled, but even so.

Every time I put on sunblock, for example, which I must do to walk over to the raw foods store seven avenue blocks away and return the bottles, I think about the hole in the earth's ozone layer over the Antarctic, and how this is happening in part due to the carbon emissions emitted by "human activity"—refrigeration, air-conditioning, hair spray—a night out in the eighties, basically. The hole was larger than the Antarctic but has shrunk to its smallest size in a decade, thanks to the banning of CFCs. This is good. It is a sign we might save the earth from global warming also.

But this reminds me of the ice caps having melted at the North Pole, which is why drilling companies now want to drill the Arctic (was it even their plan all along?) and how this melting alone could unleash an extinction-level event by releasing the giant cloud of methane gas. Which these drilling companies see as a "gold mine." It is a gas mine, though—I wish it were gold, because then it couldn't kill us. In my mind it is like a vast cloud made of all of the dead creatures of that era millions of years ago, trapped angrily beneath the earth, where they protected us forever by being hidden, and as we try to take them to the surface to burn them for fuel they run everywhere, suffocating all life, a vast ghostly cloud made of the burned dead that is turning into our deaths.

As I cover every bit of exposed skin I remember how as a child I used to fear being made to wear a special suit, the suit scientists then predicted we'd need in order to protect ourselves from solar radiation. This, of course, is why I wear a "swim shirt" at the beach now, with solar protection built in—I was always burning at the spot in the middle of my back that I couldn't quite reach and I didn't want, years later, to be told that I'd doomed myself to skin cancer for going to the beach in my twenties and thirties by myself when I was between relationships and didn't ask anyone to put sunblock on that one spot.

Will I wear the swim shirt when the water covers the land?

My longstanding commitment to sunblock was shaken recently. I was in Canada, at a Canadian Sephora looking for a favorite brand, and I asked the counter person if they carried it. The counter person said, in a soft voice, "We don't carry that one." I said, "But you do in the U.S." He said, "If you can't find American brands here it's because they failed Canada's testing standards." And when I didn't react right away the counter person added, "American brands often make claims that are false, and as the FDA in the U.S. can't afford to test them all, they fail when they come to us, as we test all of them, and then we can't sell them."

I have joined a gym because it has a pool and a sunroof that opens in warm weather. I don't go swimming, not yet. But at least, in the era of the swim shirt, wearing a shirt in

the water doesn't mean necessarily you are fat.

ON THE THIRD DAY OF THE cleanse, it feels like nothing can lie to me. I feel full of righteous fury—here, the rage, it is here!—and when, on a sidewalk full of umbrellas in the rain, heads down, someone strikes me with the edge of his umbrella, carried so low he can't see where he's going, I shout at the culprit, who passes on, saying nothing. Everyone turns to look at me except him.

What are you cleansing, he might ask, if he had stopped. And why? If he had asked, I would have told him I am hoping to get rid of the things that are in that sad American sunblock. I am hoping to rid myself of, say, Bisphenol A, also called BPA, outlawed in Europe, but approved by the FDA forty years ago, before it was tested, like many American things. Bisphenol A is now well-studied, and shown to contribute to cancer, obesity, learning disorders, and reproductive problems, which I think is a euphemism for sterility at the least. At my most cynical I imagine our corporate overlords deliberately feeding all of us an additive that they hope makes us less able to fight back. BPAs are found in the lining of American canned goods, American plastic bottles and containers, cashier receipts, cosmetics. Its use is widespread, which is why banning it is unpopular, because it would be "expensive" to get it banned. In the meantime, then, the cost of having cancer or a learning disability or a reproductive problem or of moving all of us to a new planet is passed along to consumers, as it usually is.

There's not really a way to get it out of me, though, or out of you, I would tell him, my new friend. To undertake a cleanse is to feel, briefly, like a sponge wrung clean. Before you are dropped back into the Gowanus Canal again. But perhaps it matters, those few minutes the cells are clean.

That Himalayan moss, if it is harvested in the Himalayas, is covered in jet fuel that falls out of the sky with the rain.

Come with me now, I might say to him. For if we'd only talked, surely we'd be friends. Come with me now and get a shake.

YES, BY DAY FOUR I AM PURE rage. But it is okay because I am unable and basically unwilling to speak to anyone but Dustin, my partner, in person, and I don't talk about any of this.

A bag of Doritos on a subway platform newsstand is suddenly the most appealing siren. I stand in front of it, aching, until the train takes me away.

How do we survive ourselves, I want to ask the rich vegetarians in the store again, as I return my package of containers. The place I am getting the cleanse from sells a fantasy of a pristine world apart from this one, but there is no world apart. There is only the world.

A Chinese tech billionaire on Weibo—China's version of Twitter—made an uproar when he Weibo'd to his fellow rich people, "The cancer we will all die from because the world is so polluted doesn't care that you are rich," or something to this effect. A rich person had stopped bothering to pretend his wealth could protect him from the dangers we all face.

China's pollution problems have been created out of their massive industrialization, as most of us know. As the American rich have destroyed their middle class, China has created a middle class with a population the size of the entire United States. Do they cleanse?

I went to China for the first time last year, where I saw Shanghai hotels, each seemingly richer than the last before it. Luxury in America is coach class in China. Shanghai luxury makes American luxury look like a hobo village. For the purposes of economics, America is the new Philippines now. China is the new America. This isn't a realization born out of the cleanse, though; it was born in the lobbies of those Shanghai hotels.

What do the rich vegans in China eat, I wonder, as I go to sleep after my last smoothie. I bet it is amazing. I forgot to check while in Shanghai, because the pork was too delicious.

———

DAY FIVE. I TELL MYSELF ABOUT "fed, not full," the sort of calm contented feeling you get when you have eaten well but not too much. I have not managed to stay off coffee. It was too much. This is my only cheat and perhaps it has ruined everything, but there it is.

It is almost time to return to normal—to everything else besides the coffee. I have fantasies of continuing. I examine the packages with glee as I consume them, even as the ordinary version of myself scoffs.

You're ridiculous, Ordinary Alex tells Cleanse Alex. You know what's next.

At some point in stores like Whole Foods, the packages of organic meats and vegetables began to be fewer in number, and were replaced with meat covered in stickers that read "No Antibiotics" or "Vegetarian Feed" or "No Pesticides." You could buy "local," which means "not shipped by burning so much jet fuel it would get even into that awesome Himalayan moss," but which also usually means "covered in pesticide somewhere in New Jersey, most likely a pesticide banned in Europe."

So many bargains.

I want to find that seven billionth child and tell him to run for his life, but where should he go? Where do we all go?

I will never be a thin rich vegan, I have accepted this. Have they? If you think petroleum products are vegan, are you thinking back far enough? The counter clerk who takes back my last containers is optimistic and kind as I make bland claims about how great it was and how I want to continue. I cast a last look at the cost of the smoothies and the raw lasagna and the dried kale and the Himalayan salt—is there anything left in the Himalayas?—and then return to my life.

I have lost five pounds.

Dak Dori Tang, Island Style

What is a cleanse, really? What are we trying to get rid of? Usually, for me, it's been a sense of being alienated from my own body. I can't sustain the sort of cleanse my brother had me try, and I think our best efforts come from what we can make a part of our daily lives. And so I turn here to Korean food.

When my mother was in Korea with me during my childhood, she became quite sick with tuberculosis, and then, during her recovery, became pregnant with my brother. Her doctors there encouraged her to go home and eat the food she'd grown up with to help her recover. She did, and my brother, whether this matters or not, is a very healthy man.

Having spent my first three years of life in Korea, I wanted to try cooking Korean food myself, in part because I was tired of spending so much money on it and also because I wanted to follow a taste. This soup is something I found, if not cleansing, exactly, then deeply consoling, and perhaps that is better than a "cleanse," though the pepper will also sweat out most colds, as I've found, and a flu too.

1 good-size piece of
    kombu, probably about
    4 to 6 inches, simmered
    in a quart of water
1 white onion
3 to 4 cloves of garlic,
    chopped or smashed, as
    you prefer
1 tablespoon neutral oil,
    such as grapeseed oil
8 to 10 pieces of chicken,
    preferably dark meat, or
    a whole chicken in parts
2 tablespoons Korean chili
    flake, coarse

2 tablespoons Korean chili
    flake, fine
soy sauce or tamari to
    taste—I'd say about 1 to 2
    tablespoons
2 tablespoons kochujang
    (Korean red pepper
    paste)
1 tablespoon honey or agave
1 to 2 large sweet potatoes
¼ to ½ of a green cabbage,
    sliced thin
2 scallions, chopped
1 tablespoon toasted
    sesame seeds

Start your kombu broth in a large pot. Meanwhile, in a separate pot, chop the onion and garlic and sauté them in the oil on low to low-medium heat, until they're soft and translucent.

Turn the heat up to medium and add the chicken, letting it brown for about 3 minutes on each side.

Then pour in the broth, and add the chili flake, soy sauce or tamari, and kochujang.

Note: I use the two kinds of flake plus the paste because they each bring something to the dish—the result is a layered hot pepper flavor that never overwhelms. The kochujang has miso in it also, which matters. For extra hotness, add a dash of chili oil and some chopped jalapeño.

Stir in the honey or agave. Bring to a boil and then simmer. After about 10 minutes, when the chicken meat has turned white, add the chopped sweet potatoes and cabbage, and cover it. You can also add white potato if you like, or kale too—kale is excellent in this. Carrot is good in here as well.

Cook for at least 15 more minutes at a simmer, stirring occasionally. I recommend you turn the heat down very low if you like and cook it covered for a half hour or more, so the collagen from the chicken gets into the soup and the flavors intensify.

Serve with fresh rice, brown or white, or as is. Top with the chopped scallions and the toasted sesame seeds. For extra fun: add a little more water to make it more soup-like and less stewy if you like. That way, after you've eaten all the chicken out of it, you can use the broth the next day to poach eggs in and eat it over the leftover rice for breakfast, which is just great.

CALCULATED DESTRUCTION

POROCHISTA KHAKPOUR

Porochista Khakpour is the author of the critically acclaimed memoir *Sick*; the novel *The Last Illusion*, a 2014 Best Book of the Year, according to NPR, *Kirkus Reviews*, *BuzzFeed*, and many more publications; and her debut novel *Sons and Other Flammable Objects*, a *New York Times* Editor's Choice and the 2007 California Book Award winner in the First Fiction category. Born in Tehran and raised in the Los Angeles area, she is mostly based in New York City.

One of my favorite Persian proverbs goes, "When the tide of misfortune moves over you, even jelly will break your teeth." I've only met one person who didn't like the Persian creation *tahdig*—literally meaning "bottom of the pot," the crispy near-burnt rice that's akin to the crust in a burnt pot of rice, but better—and that was because he once broke a tooth on a particularly jagged and charred piece. I've told this story to more than a few Iranians who mainly shrug (*some might say it was worth it*, an older relative muttered) or chuckle softly. *Tahdig* is so beloved, some might say it matters more than certain people do.

In these seasons of nonstop geopolitical atrocities, beginning with the Paris attacks and H.R. 158 and sanctions in Iran, the Muslim world, and certainly Iran, has been headed for a bad time. Even with the Iran nuclear deal, the world of the Supreme Leader and clerics was never going to gel well with this America. Then add the forty-fifth president to this mix! All in all, it has been a time of considerable anxiety for Iranian Americans—or at the very least, this Iranian American.

Yet Persian food, I've always maintained, is comfort food. I'm biased of course as an Iranian refugee who clung to kebab long before burgers. But with its few spices and ample herbs, it's fairly easy on the palate, all about aroma and freshness—greens both raw and cooked, stews and kebabs, yogurts, breads, and of course, rice. Rice is not the vessel for other good things as it is in many cultures, but quite often the main attraction, you might say. Iranian people take an absurd amount of pride in their rice. We're talking heaping plates of basmati rice cooked in oil and then, once served, lovingly patted down with butter. If you're lucky it will be smudged in saffron, maybe even topped with sumac if in the company of its perfect companion the kebab. *Polo* (Farsi for "rice") is meant to be a decadent experience—Iranians know it's not particularly good for you, and almost all the most well-known Persian restaurants of my native LA's Persian enclave Tehrangeles offer salad substitutes now. It's a sort of sacrilege, but dieting Tehrangelenos know their downfall. Iranians revere rice, and this Iranian is no exception.

"I felt like something of a crazed witch as I hovered over my pot, gingerly poking the bottom with a fork, hoping for a crispiness that went beyond caramelized glass."
—Porochista Khakpour

A few years ago, I came down with all sorts of health problems related to my Lyme disease, and I had to take so many tests, including a test for food allergies. It turns out that I have three: coffee, green beans, and *rice*. This was of dire concern to my family. First of all, had I been poisoning myself my whole life? How had I not known? The doctor maintained it was a very mild level of allergy and that really the tests were not that accurate. *So I can eat rice?* I demanded, more than asked. She paused and said, *Well, I'd avoid it mostly. But if you have to, well, you will live.*

Living without rice does not make much sense to Iranians. And so I ignored the diagnosis, and in fact, former rice addict that I am, I became even more obsessed with it. It felt temptingly illicit—a treat that would lead to bad things, but that's what a treat is, at least to me.

I've loved rice my whole life, but I only recently decided it was time to learn not only how to cook it, but how to properly burn it. To learn how, I began with the source, my mother, who made it sound simple in her text message:

Tahdig

1 cup rice
2 cups water
salt and oil

"Wash rice. Put the washed rice into a pan, mix water and salt and oil, and bring them to boil. Let it boil till all the water is gone. Bring the heat to very low. Cover and let it cook for half an hour. The more you cook it, the thicker *tahdig* you will have. ☺ ☺ ☺"

But this method never worked for me.

The internet will get more technical than your mother, who wants to make it for you anyway, who sees no point in you trying to do something she can do better. It will tell you to use a heavy-bottom pot, and to only add three to four tablespoons of salt to the water, then to boil for five minutes only before you put it on medium or medium-high heat, while in a small bowl you better get to melting butter (about one tablespoon of butter per cup of dry rice) with a pinch of saffron in it (preferably ground with a mortar and pestle). My mother would be clearly rolling her eyes at this point. Then you go about poking three to four holes into the top of the rice and pouring the butter down the holes, afterward placing three layers of paper towels to cover the top of the pan and cooking at medium to medium-high heat for exactly eight minutes. Next, the internet suggests you turn the stove down to the lowest temperature it will go and steam for exactly thirty-five more minutes. My mother thinks these numbers are insane and so American.

Finally, the internet will remind you, it's not over—you can still mess all your hard work up! Even serving is a crisis: you have to carefully scoop the rice out from the top of the pan being sure not to break the crust on the bottom. Once all the rice is out except for the crust, take another plate big enough to cover the opening of the pan and flip the crust out onto the plate, where it better be golden and brown and just burnt enough to be crisp but not qualify as actually burnt. The

internet will tell you that you can eventually advance to using sliced rounds of potato or pita (preferably Persian lavash bread) on the bottom of the pan before you sprinkle in the boiled rice, like your mother also did perfectly.

There are other methods too, that involve special pots, yogurt paste, and all sorts of numbers and even more magical thinking, but one thing I have learned is that *tahdig* will never be perfect. You will always wish it was just a little bit one way or another, though an equal universal truth to *tahdig*: those who consume it will always be charmed without fail.

Every *tahdig* is uniquely its own mess. That to me seems apt for the Persian psyche as well: the constant striving for something that is essentially unattainable and utterly imperfect in its essence anyway. But in a time when being Iranian is not easy in this country or even in Iran, there is something very satisfying in taking part in this ritual of cooking that is less about loving creation than calculated destruction. I felt like something of a crazed witch as I hovered over my pot, gingerly poking the bottom with a fork, with hope for a crispiness that went beyond caramelized glass. I wanted to create something that could break and be broken, to make something cumbersome and hard out of something that's so often fluffy and easy. I wanted rice that was nearly a weapon it was so corrupted. I wanted the possibility of losing a tooth, of ruining a pan at the very least. Even better than that, I wanted the exercise in never quite getting there.

Part of the lesson of *tahdig* is that while we think it's easy to destroy something, our investment in preservation outdoes our instinct to demolish. Our rice may be corroded, our carbohydrates just a little bit deadly—we deserve it, all of us really.

DEPRESSION PANCAKES

MAILE MELOY

Maile Meloy is the author of the novels *Do Not Become Alarmed*, *Liars and Saints*, and *A Family Daughter*; the story collections *Half in Love* and *Both Ways Is the Only Way I Want It*, which was named one of *The New York Times'* Best Books of the Year; and the Apothecary middle-grade trilogy. She has received *The Paris Review*'s Aga Khan Prize, the PEN/Malamud Award, the American Academy of Arts and Letters' Rosenthal Family Foundation Award, and a Guggenheim Fellowship. Born in Helena, Montana, she now lives in Los Angeles.

When my grandfather, Pete, was living on his own during the Great Depression, his mother, Carrie, sent him a few recipes he could make cheaply for himself. One was for shredded carrot salad. One was for pancakes, "enough for two unless they are very big eaters." She assumed that he could learn to cook, in his twenties, and hoped he would have someone to eat with.

Pete had grown up on a drought-ravaged ranch in western Montana. He was round and thoughtful and optimistic. His older brother, Hank, was lean and brooding and handsome. Hank moved to New York to be a painter, and sent money home for Pete to go to college, even when he was broke himself. They had a sister in between them, Caroline, who followed Hank to New York to find work. When she told her father, a Roosevelt

Democrat, that she'd fallen in love with a man in New York, he said, "I'll bet he's a damned dirty Republican." Caroline said, "No, he's a socialist." Her father didn't know what to say to that.

Pete, the youngest, stayed in Montana. I don't know if he ever made the pancakes. He ran for local office while still in college, campaigning on horseback, but lost. He directed plays, and played Sir Toby Belch in *Twelfth Night*. He convinced a shy, lonely kid in his dorm to play Andrew Aguecheek, drawing him out into success and friendship, a story that made Pete cry when he told it at eighty.

Hank came home from New York to visit, and the two brothers made pottery. They dug up clay on the ranch and made their own glazes. They tried firing the plates in the blacksmith's kiln but that was too hot, so they went to the local brickmaker and asked if they could use his kilns. That brickyard is now the Archie Bray Foundation for the Ceramic Arts, which Pete

helped found. He went to law school after college and became a tax lawyer and then a district judge. He was a devoted Democrat like his father, and he used to send me absentee ballots when I was in college, to make sure I voted in every election.

Pete met my grandmother, Harriett, one of the most independent women I've ever known, when she was working at the Industrial Accidents Board in Helena, Montana. She'd grown up in North Dakota and was younger than Pete; the banks started failing when she was thirteen. Her father, who worked in a beleaguered bank, sent her alone in the family car to the next town with a bag of cash. Men with guns would have held her father up, but he didn't think they would bother a child, and she had already taught herself to drive. She delivered the cash, stayed the night with an aunt and uncle, and drove back in the morning.

Her own Welsh granny had managed to get a university degree

in the nineteenth century. I didn't understand why that was such a source of pride for my grandmother, because I thought all women went to college. Harriett was the chair of the Montana Board of Education and the librarian at the Montana Historical Society, and she used to quiz me about grammar and the importance of art classes in school. You did not say "lay" in her presence when you meant "lie." She kept working after Pete retired, and people who knew her from boards and planning commissions sometimes didn't know she was married.

Harriett and Pete had five children, including a set of twins, and my grandfather never—that I know of—cooked a family meal, not even a pancake breakfast. Harriett made dinner every night. Pete had dug pottery clay from the ground and made his own glazes, but I don't think he ever made a shredded carrot salad.

If Carrie, my great-grandmother, had culinary hopes for her son, they skipped a generation. In college, my father shared a house with his younger brother, who didn't cook, so my father learned how and liked it. He made dinner for us all the time—spaghetti, lasagna, enchiladas, giant salads, corn on the cob from the garden—and I grew up thinking that was what men did. My brother is the cook at his house, and makes his own pizza dough and ferments pickles. I married a man who learned to cook from his own father, and he's much better at it than I am. I happily ceded that territory to him.

This is the recipe as Carrie wrote it out in her headlong cursive. She thought Pete would have sour milk on hand, and might not have access to an egg. I use buttermilk and the egg, double the recipe for breakfast guests—or triple it if they are very big eaters—and put whipped cream and berries on top. My brother uses yogurt and milk instead of buttermilk, and a second egg, and his pancakes are fluffier than mine, and (honestly) better.

Depression Pancakes

1 cup flour

1 teaspoon salt

1 tablespoon sugar

sour milk or buttermilk

baking soda

hot water

1 egg

Combine 1 cup flour, 1 teaspoon salt, and 1 tablespoon sugar. Mix smooth and rather stiff with sour milk or buttermilk.

Put one teaspoon of baking soda a little better than level full in a cup and pour some hot water on it—maybe a quarter of a cup of hot water. Stir until dissolved. Pour this in batter and stir well by beating; thin down with sour milk until it will pour from spoon or pitcher or whatever you mix it in. The addition of an egg well beaten helps them but they are good enough without the egg.

If you want to increase this recipe, just use more flour and more salt, sugar, and soda.

AUTHENTIC AFRICAN COOKING

JEFFERY RENARD ALLEN

Jeffery Renard Allen is the author of five books, including two collections of poetry, *Harbors and Spirits* and *Stellar Places*, and the novels *Rails Under My Back*, which won *The Chicago Tribune*'s Heartland Prize for Fiction, and *Song of the Shank*, which was a finalist for the PEN/Faulkner Award and nominated for the Dublin Literary Prize. His short story collection *Holding Pattern* won the Ernest J. Gaines Award for Literary Excellence. Allen's collection of stories *Fat Time* will be published in 2020. He lives in Charlottesville, Virginia, where he is Professor of Creative Writing at the University of Virginia.

My wife suffered through many hard times on the island of Zanzibar where she was born and raised. Of the many stories she's told me, I would like to share this one. My wife was living on her own and had just started a new job, a good thing. The problem, she had no money to buy food and no food to eat at home. Thankfully, a neighbor came to her aid, a young Muslim woman who for a full month invited my wife into her home three times a day to enjoy a simple meal.

Similar customs of feeding the hungry are common throughout sub-Saharan Africa. For example, in some parts of Nigeria, a homeless person can walk into a restaurant or café and get a meal on the house. One can provide a meal for the less fortunate because staples like fufu, ugali, and rice are inexpensive compared to meat and fish. If it takes a village to raise a child, it also takes a village to feed a hungry belly. Most people in sub-Saharan Africa engage in a daily struggle for survival, and for that reason they've had to develop clever and creative culinary practices to stave off hunger, even starvation.

Some years ago, I spent a summer month on Lamu off the Kenyan coast through the help of two good friends in Nairobi who wanted to start a writers' residency on the island. I was the ideal test subject given my fondness for the place. Lamu feels like a throwback to another time with its houses erected from stone and winding narrow streets. You get where you need to go by foot or donkey or *jahazi* (*dhow*) powered by outboard motors since there are no motorized vehicles on the island with the exception of a motorcycle or two. You relish in the slow pace and the air from the Indian Ocean, free of any worries about crime or violence—this would later change— and relieved that no one will try to hustle or game you. Lamu is the perfect place to get away and write for month (or two) as long as you don't mind a bit of donkey shit.

I stayed inside a tower-like structure that was the British owner's take on the traditional Swahili home, a vacation house built to impress guests rather than provide comfort. My time there felt a bit like camping out inside an art installation. The owner, whom I never met, left the residence in the care of his "house boy," a local man named Saidi (Friday), a short, slight, and slim man in his early thirties who wore a fez as evidence of his Islamic faith, and to offset his preference for Western-style shirts and jeans.

Saidi was an outstanding cook. I only took coffee in the mornings, but after Saidi had brewed a fresh pot, I would give him fifteen dollars to spend at the market on the fresh meat, fish, fruits, and vegetables that he needed to prepare my lunch and dinner. For lunch I would usually eat a whole grilled snapper with some tasty side dishes. For dinner, chicken or beef smothered in an exotic sauce that had been passed on to Saidi at some point from a Swiss chef. The environs where Saidi served my meals were as pleasing as the food. I sat at a table in the open court with the full sky in view overhead. Turtles swam in the pond at the center of the court. Each night, Saidi took care to light a mosquito coil at the foot of my table so I could enjoy my dinner undisturbed.

Saidi always purchased and cooked more food than I could eat. I'm certain he took the extras home to his wife and son. In fact, one morning he told me, "I'm out of spice," prompting me to give him double the usual, although I knew that he would spend only a few dollars on turmeric, ginger, cardamom, and other spices. Saidi was adept at taking care of his own. Each day a young guy named Mohammed came to the house to help Saidi cook, an arrangement that allowed Saidi to feed Mohammed, enjoy his company, and also train him as a chef.

One night about two weeks into my stay, I took my place at the table as usual, and Saidi lit the mosquito coil, but rather than go upstairs to retrieve my dinner from the kitchen,

> "While it might seem that West African cooking has a secret history, the foreign influences on the East African diet appear to be in plain view."
>
> – Jeffery Renard Allen

he simply stood at the table for a moment looking at me. "I'm going to give you something different tonight," he said. "I'm going to show you how we Swahili eat." He took the stairs two at a time as was his wont and carefully made his way back down with a plate in one hand and a large salad bowl in the other. He set these items on the table. On the plate, a half loaf of sliced white bread. Inside the bowl, chunks of baked white potatoes. "Now this is how we Swahilis eat," he said. He smiled at me, bemused.

So I went about eating, wrapping cold chunks of potato inside the cold bread. Suffice it to say, I had my doubts about the authenticity of this meal. Surely Saidi had simply pocketed my money, then, tongue-in-cheek, prepared me this flavorless dish. How likely is it that potato and white bread combination has a place in the traditional Swahili diet? This dish has a long-established place in

Swahili gastronomy, but that is only half the story. The foreign forces who tried to subjugate and exploit sub-Saharan Africans through slavery and colonialism also provided many of the food sources that sustain people on the continent today.

To start, potatoes are indigenous to Peru and Bolivia. The Spanish introduced the tuber to Europe and the Canary Islands off the African coast in the sixteenth century. Then, in the seventeenth century, the Dutch brought the tuber to what is now South Africa. However, the potato didn't fully make its way into the continental diet until the period of European conquest in the 1880s when missionaries and colonists brought the root to the new colonies. Even today, Irish farmers who established the potato industry in Nigeria still operate it in the city of Jos.

But the potato is only the tip of the iceberg. Of the seven main staple foods in sub-Saharan Africa—maize, rice, yams, cassava, beans, sorghum, and millet—only sorghum, millet, and yams are indigenous to the continent. As we know, Spanish explorers first encountered maize in the New World in 1492. They carried it back to Europe, and from there it was introduced to other parts of the globe. Most bean varieties on the continent today stem from either Mesoamerica, where they were first domesticated thousands of years ago, or from Asia. What about cassava? Although Nigeria is the world's largest producer of cassava—a central ingredient used to make that celebrated West African dish, fufu—cassava is native to South America. Portuguese traders from Brazil brought the crop to the African continent in the sixteenth century.

Nigeria and Ghana are both famous from their groundnut stew. The only problem, these stews are not actually made from groundnut, the indigenous West African Bambara bean, but with peanuts, which Portuguese traders brought to the continent from Brazil in the 1500s. (This does not change the fact that the best peanuts I've ever tasted I purchased on the streets of Lagos, where vendors sell them in reused liquor bottles.) Cashew stews are also popular in West Africa. Once again, the Portuguese are to blame. They transported cashews from Brazil to Mozambique in the 1500s, where the nut made its way to other regions of the continent.

While it might seem that West African cooking has a secret history, the foreign influences on the East African diet appear to be in plain view given the widespread consumption of Indian dishes like pilau (spiced rice), samosa, and chapatti across the region. I have come to know this cuisine well in the years following that month I spent on Lamu. My wife, Zawadi, is Tanzanian, and although Zawadi's family comes from the village of Kigoma on the mainland, Zawadi was born and raised on Zanzibar, another Swahili stronghold in the Indian Ocean. Most Tanzanians are poor and struggle to make ends meet, so few people can afford to eat meat or fish every day. The typical diet consists of bread or mandazi (a triangular doughnut) and tea for breakfast, ugali (maize flour) with beans for lunch, and rice and green bananas for dinner, foods that, for the most part, don't originate on the continent.

People do what they can to savor a treat here or there in the form of mishkaki (beef skewers), chips (fried potatoes), boiled peanuts, grilled corn, or a tasty fruit like jackfruit, lychee, durian, passion fruit, papaya, to say nothing of mangoes. (Some facts: mangoes were first grown in the Indian subcontinent. Persian traders brought them to East Africa in the tenth century. Then, at the start of the Atlantic Slave Trade in the fifteenth century, the Portuguese brought them to West Africa.)

The most popular type of rice in Tanzania is Mbeya, named after the city where it is grown, although basmati, jasmine, and other forms of rice are common. Need I say that despite the widespread consumption of rice across the continent, non-Africans played a crucial role in establishing the grain as staple, notwithstanding the fact that rice was cultivated in the Niger River delta in ancient times, between 1500 and 800 BC, with crops extending as far as present-day Senegal. For whatever reason cultivation ceased. Then, during the Atlantic Slave Trade, both the Portuguese (again!)

and the Dutch took Asiatic rice to their respective colonies in West Africa. Interestingly enough, from there it came to the New World via traders and slaves.

In fact, Black slaves taught their white masters how to grow and cook rice here in America. (Might this be one reason that the iconic logo for Uncle Ben's rice depicts an elderly black man?) Black slaves introduced other important foods to the American cuisine, including the watermelon, black-eyed peas, and okra, which are all indigenous to Africa. Black slaves also pioneered the vernacular misnomer "yam" for the sweet potato. And some might be surprised to learn that the West African kola nut remains the base ingredient for Coca-Cola and Pepsi, the component which gives these carbonated soft drinks their distinctive taste.

Of course, these kinds of cultural exchanges have been going on forever. Appropriation is an undeniable fact of human interaction. What we take from others we make our own and in so doing craft a unique transformation. Put differently, the local preparation of a "stolen" food or dish is a valid and varied matter involving repurposing and improvisation, a home-grown style, in much the same way that the universally celebrated musical form jazz involves playing idiomatically distinct "black" music on European instruments. To take an example or two, when East Africans make chapatti, they add coconut milk in place of water, giving their version of the bread a distinct taste. And what we call grits here in America is a form of porridge across East Africa, except that there, the locals mix in peanuts to provide flavor and much-needed protein.

I'm always curious to see how my wife will respond to American versions of certain foods she knows from back home. With this in mind, a few months ago I decided to take her to the Waffle House here in Charlottesville to try grits. Not surprisingly, she found it bland, tasteless. I told her, "To make it taste good, you have to smother it in butter and sugar."

Despite my own naughty experiments, Tanzanian givens like rice and ugali remain essential in our household. Still, I continually seek ways to amuse my wife. I often tell her that ugali comes from *here*. But, playing the good husband, I also try to introduce her to other maize dishes that I cook up from time to time, things I have picked up in my travels around the continent like this South African cornbread. Perhaps my recipe will catch on here in America.

Mealie Bread (South African Corn Bread)

½ cup milk
¼ cup salted and melted
    butter
2 eggs
1 cup unbleached all-purpose
    flour
1 cup cornmeal

2 tablespoons sugar
2 teaspoons baking powder
1 teaspoon salt
½ teaspoon paprika
2 cups of yellow corn kernels
    (thaw if frozen; cut the
    kernels off the cob if fresh)

Preheat oven to 350°F. Butter/grease an 8½-by-4½-inch loaf tin.

Place all the ingredients except one cup of corn kernels into your blender and pulse until the batter comes together. Add the remaining cup of corn kernels and pulse a few times to mix the kernels into the batter. Pour the batter into the prepared pan.

Bake the bread for 50 to 55 minutes, or until a toothpick inserted into the center comes out clean.

Cool the bread in the pan for 3 to 5 minutes before turning the bread out onto a wire rack to continue cooling.

Serve warm.

GRIEF PICKLES

KRISTEN ISKANDRIAN

Kristen Iskandrian's debut novel *Motherest* was long-listed for the Center for Fiction First Novel Prize and chosen as a monthly pick by *Vanity Fair*, *The Millions*, Shondaland, and *The Wall Street Journal*, as well as being named a Best Book of the Year by *Publishers Weekly* and *Lenny Letter*. Her short fiction has appeared or is forthcoming in *The O. Henry Prize Stories 2014*, *The Best American Short Stories 2018*, *Tin House*, *McSweeney's Quarterly Concern*, *Ploughshares*, *Joyland*, and *Zyzzyva*, among others. She lives in Birmingham, Alabama. For more information, visit kristeniskandrian.com.

I have this vision of myself at about ten years old riding a loop around our driveway on my bike one-handed. In my other hand I hold a pickle. Nothing gourmet, not even a Claussen—most likely a Vlasic, its muddy, warty green some kind of F-you to the prosaic blitheness of summer, its hefty salt the antithesis of the arguably more popular one-handed summer food, the ice cream cone. I take tiny bites, wanting to make my pickle last. It is a way of being alone and a way of keeping time: when I finish the pickle, I'll know what to do next. I don't want the pickle to be over.

There are foods we enjoy because they taste good; they ingratiate themselves with immediacy to the pleasure-centers of our palate, whether for their sweetness or their saltiness or their inarguable succulence. These foods offer a straightforward sensory experience almost like a call-and-response—key in the lock, lid to the jar, *when*

*I say "uh," you say "ah."** The pickle may be one of these foods for some people—it certainly is for me—but I think, more interestingly, there are also categories of foods that we love for more nebulous or romantic or even genetic reasons. Foods of our forbears, foods that we see ourselves in.

In this case: I am the pickle. The pickle is me. In their preparation, they are a quintessential alone food. I identify with their need for solitude, their sometimes divisive quality.

As a kid I was vaguely embarrassed by my love for them; I'd stare at my friends' plates where pickles that had come on a burger or with a sandwich were pushed unceremoniously to the side, not confident enough to ask if I could have them (though I desperately wanted them). Years later, in high school, I forged a lifelong bond with my friend Jessica over a jar of pickles and a drained can of tuna with a bunch of mayonnaise—pungent snacks

we'd previously only eaten alone. My husband loathed pickles when we met; I've since converted him to the allure of pucker and vinegar. I can't think of anything more straightforwardly delightful and satisfying than a good pickle, or even a mediocre pickle, and I love them in all forms, from twelve-dollar artisan plates at fancy restaurants to dusty jars of Mt. Olive at the corner store.

The earliest pickles I knew were *torshi*, the Farsi word for pickle, although my family hails from Iraq, not Iran. My mostly German grandmother married an Assyrian man and, after immigrating to Mosul, learned to prepare many Middle Eastern specialties. My Armenian father, born and raised in Baghdad and the parent, I think, from whom my love of tart, acidic things stems, particularly loved *amba*, a pickled mango condiment that not even my grandmother knew how to make—we'd get jars shipped from my aunt in Chicago who had access to an impressive Middle Eastern grocery. When I was very young, the bright orange, turmeric-flecked

---

* "Let Me Clear My Throat," DJ Kool.

tongues of mango repulsed me—I didn't even know what mango *was*, let alone turmeric—until I one day got brave and took a bite from my dad's sandwich, a pita stuffed with *amba* and hard-boiled egg. It was delicious. I couldn't deny it. And it made me feel weirdly close to him, us two against the world, or at least, the other three members of our family who pushed the jar away in disgust.

My grandmother's *torshi* was a different matter. She'd fill enormous jars with vegetables—some with chunks of turnip and a few beets, for color, and others with carrots, cauliflower, and celery—and then add water and a bit of vinegar and a lot of salt, seal the jars, and place them under the sink. I'd get used to opening the cabinet for a paper towel or a new sponge and seeing them there, tucked in the back, those eerie aquariums of color and salt, busily fermenting. "Close the door, close it," Omi would say. "They need darkness."

I would sneak tastes before they were "ready," their readiness something alchemical and arbitrary to me, an impatient kid who wanted pickles, but to my grandmother, I'm sure, their readiness was a matter of timing and instinct honed over many years and batches. After maybe five days or a week, she'd taste and say "not quite," shoving them back into the dark. Even half-pickled pickles were pickle enough for me; I loved the still-raw crunch. But Omi knew when they'd reached their apotheosis, and I would eat piece after piece until I was scolded to stop, great thirst often cited as a serious consequence for pickle gluttony.

Seclusion, and darkness: two things I crave in my adult life, my writing life. You are what you eat, as they say.

As a stressed-out PhD student, I discovered a recipe for quick pickles, and a trap door opened in my food-memory consciousness. I recalled reading the label of the grocery store pickle jar as a ten-year-old kid, thinking if I just had cucumbers, water, distilled vinegar, salt, calcium chloride, polysorbate 80, natural flavor, yellow 5—I could *make* a Vlasic. It had never occurred to me at any point during my adult life that I could *make* Omi's *torshi*. She'd died more than ten years before, and it was as though she'd taken it with her. To my surprise, quick pickling was easy and enjoyable; my stress evaporated in the steaming brine, which did not, it turned out, require the final four items from the Vlasic label, and afterward, looking at the rows of cooling jars of carrots, green beans, and cauliflower, I felt a calm sense of accomplishment. Less than twenty-four hours later, we had legitimate pickles.

Around that time, my dear friend Sabrina gave me one of several enormous jars of homemade pickles that she would set aside for me over the years, when she felt moved to make them. They were the closest in taste and texture and appearance to my grandmother's, and the jar alone, just the sight of it, made me feel connected to Sabrina and to my grandmother and to the idea that friendship, at its best, is also a fermentation, a commingling of histories and bloodlines, a ripening of self.

From that point on, the urge to make pickles was strong and precise, and always seemed to follow or occur during—as if in response to—some great sadness or bitter disappointment. More than once I wondered if anyone had ever tried using their own tears as brine, wondered if our proclivity for salt in some way mirrors our own bodily ecosystem.

A couple of years ago I was experiencing a lot of sorrow for a variety of reasons: my mom, who is ill, had just returned home from a stint in the hospital, and I didn't know how to be helpful, or how to even witness her suffering. It was painful to see my dad struggle to care for her too. It was a moment of feeling suspended between my life as a needful daughter and my life as an adult, a mother, a caretaker; a moment of confronting and interrogating my needs and weird furies. I felt hopelessly out of bandwidth. At home, I had a crisper drawer full of languishing vegetables, reminders of meals I was supposed to have made, and the sight of them made me feel like even more of a failure. Without a recipe or even a specific plan, I started peeling and chopping. In a pot on the stove I added water, vinegar, a few crushed cloves of garlic, a bit of brine from a jar of pickled jalapeños, and a lot of kosher salt. I didn't measure anything. I let it all come to a boil and then poured it over the jars of vegetables. I wiped down the refrigerator drawers, happy that they were empty, feeling strangely emptied myself. The next day, our neighbor friends stopped by and it turned out that we had all had a spectacularly bad week. I opened some champagne and rummaged in the pantry for something more to serve, finding not much beyond some very unremarkable chips and cookies. And then I remembered my Grief Pickles.

We ate the alone-food together and felt, I think, less alone. Sometimes you have to celebrate sadness, too.

Quick Grief Pickles

(or, maybe more accurately: Grief Quick Pickles)

Consider this a guideline, not a hard-and-fast recipe. Let your grief guide you:

Your favorite crunchy vegetables, chopped into spears, rounds, or bite-sized pieces. I suggest carrots, cucumbers, cauliflower, green beans, radishes, singly or in any combination. Roughly enough to fill 2 16-ounce mason jars.

2 cups white vinegar

2 ¼ cups water

Between ¼ and ⅓ cup kosher salt. You can always add more salt OR more liquid, so don't worry too much about precision.

Extras, in any combination you like: 2 to 3 peeled/crushed (but still intact) garlic cloves, 1 to 2 tablespoons dill seed, 1 to 2 tablespoons sugar, red pepper flakes, fresh dill, and my favorite: a few glugs from a jar of pickled jalapeños—both the brine and a few of the actual pickles—which I always have in my refrigerator.

Fill two mason jars with your chopped vegetables. Add everything else (except fresh dill, if using) to a large non-reactive pot, and set on high.

Let it come to a boil, and then turn the heat down and simmer for 5 to 8 minutes. Taste your brine to determine if it needs more salt, more vinegar, etc. When it is to your liking, let it cool slightly, and then ladle it carefully into your waiting jars of vegetables. Keep the jars uncovered on your counter until they are completely cool—this will take a while. Once cool, you can stuff fresh dill or other herbs into your jars, screw the lids on, and store in the refrigerator. They will be delicious the next day, and then get better and better for as long as they last. If you have leftover brine, save it in a jar and store it in the refrigerator, or just chop more veggies.

Pro-tip #1: When you finish off a jar, you can add fresh raw veggies into the brine and leave them be in the refrigerator. They'll take longer to pickle and they won't be as strong, but after a couple of days they'll taste great. Tamar Adler's revelatory *An Everlasting Meal* taught me to reuse all available brine—even store-bought—and it has been a game-changer.

Pro-tip #2: Resist the urge to stick a fork that has been in your mouth back into the jar. Bacteria can spoil the brine.

SPAGHETTI AND BOOKS

BETH (BICH MINH) NGUYEN

Beth (Bich Minh) Nguyen is the author of the memoir *Stealing Buddha's Dinner*, the novel *Short Girls*, and the novel *Pioneer Girl*. Her work has received an American Book Award and a PEN/Jerard Award, among other honors, and has been featured in numerous anthologies and university and community reads programs. She currently teaches in the MFA program at the University of Wisconsin, Madison.

Sometimes I think I spent most of my childhood trying to figure out why I was Vietnamese in a white American city. Trying to figure out how I was going to get by, how to be safe from notice, how soon I could get out of there. I was a quietly stressed-out kid who didn't ask questions. But there were two things that always helped: food and books. They were a refuge for me, and my greatest joy was the chance to eat something delicious while reading something delicious.

One summer—I think I was in fourth or fifth grade—my local public library gave away bookmarks from Denny's that also served as free-meal coupons for readers under the age of twelve. Every time I checked out books, I received another bookmark. I collected a stack of them, enough to last me and my sister and brother for many months. Our family didn't go out to eat often, and never at Denny's, one of many American restaurants that sat on the commercial pass of Twenty-Eighth Street in the town of Grand Rapids, Michigan, where we lived. But my stepmother wasn't one to pass up a good deal. The bookmarked meals came with a limited menu: hamburger, hot dog, grilled cheese, spaghetti. I always chose the spaghetti. During that year of Denny's, spaghetti and books became twinned comforts.

At home, my stepmother sometimes made spaghetti by pouring a jar or can of sauce into a pan of ground beef. She said it was wasteful to eat tomato sauce without meat. She was so absolute about it that Denny's meatless spaghetti seemed a delightful transgression, one that I began to crave. And I'm pretty sure I craved it because of commercials, and the war between Ragú and Prego that raged on during the 1980s. In the commercials someone was usually ladling red sauce over a pile of spaghetti while accordion music played. It was always spaghetti, romantically twirled on a fork (which, I learned, was much harder than it looked). In the commercials, the happiness of the family depended on this sauce, this pasta, this music.

I grew up in a household of refugees who had fled Vietnam and ended up in a conservative town in the Midwest. Our lives were split between Vietnamese and American selves. The definitions of these identities were at once clear and amorphous, subject to shifts in culturally determined tastes and our own growing awareness of being two selves in almost every instance. If you were to go back in time to the kitchen from my childhood, you would see a refrigerator filled with leftover Vietnamese food, bean sprouts, fish sauce, and pickled vegetables, but also ketchup and sliced yellow cheese and Jell-O salad. In the cupboards: Ritz crackers, canned green beans, Little Debbie snack cakes; dried squid, shrimp chips. At home, it was good to eat my grandmother's stewed beef with eggs; for school, I learned to bring bologna sandwiches and pretend that I too had meatloaf for dinner the night before.

As a writer who often writes about food, I am frequently asked about the foods I like to eat and cook. People are often surprised or disappointed when my answer is *not* Vietnamese food. (The urge to essentialize is strong.) I do love Vietnamese food, but it's not what I cook at home. It's not the first cuisine I turn to when I'm stressed out and worried. Indeed, Vietnamese food sometimes reminds me too much of family and childhood and growing up in a mostly white area in Michigan—all of which can bring more complication and questioning than comfort. If I'm looking for comfort, I look for spaghetti.

And so I've had many years of spaghetti. In college, on my own, I relied on jarred tomato sauce—whatever looked the best but was not too expensive—and never added meat. There was almost nothing easier to make that resulted in so much satisfaction: the essential crush of tomato against pasta noodle, the joy of taking a fork and spoon and mixing sauce and pasta together. I didn't begin to tire of this until after graduate school, when I finally started making my own sauce. Naively, I didn't even consult a recipe first, just bought some tomatoes and garlic and onion and threw them, chopped up together, in a pan. Over the years, I learned, slowly,

to do better than that. I learned about where the ingredients came from. The order of things. How to blanch and simmer. Learning to cook better was like learning how to *be* better.

What I have here is my current version of spaghetti. It's not really a recipe but more a series of suggestions, open to as much complication or simplicity as one likes. While it can be increased and shared and adapted in all kinds of ways, it really makes a perfect solo meal—the kind of solo that is chosen and deliberate.

I tend to make this spaghetti late at night, after my kids are asleep. As ever, I read while I eat. Lately I've been making and eating this a lot. I think I've eaten a pound of spaghetti every week since the 2016 election. Each time, I hope for a small sense of progression. The sauce and the spaghetti never turn out exactly the same and I know that is how it should be. Each iteration is a bit of evolution. It is past, it is present, it is trying to look forward; it is the enduring necessity and pleasure of comfort.

Comforting Spaghetti with Tomato Sauce

YIELD: ENOUGH FOR YOU

tomatoes, whatever kind are the best where you are. As for the amount, I say use as many as you like, depending on size—maybe four or five heirlooms, maybe a whole box or more of cherry tomatoes.

¼ yellow onion

2 to 3 cloves garlic to taste

2 tablespoons olive oil

1 tablespoon butter

salt and pepper

½ cup white wine

spaghetti, about ½ pound, fresh or dried. It doesn't hurt to be particular about what kind of spaghetti you like. It doesn't hurt to get fancy sometimes. Whatever kind you get, don't overcook it.

small handful of basil or Italian parsley, chopped (optional)

fresh Parmigiano-Reggiano (optional)

Score tomatoes with an X and blanch quickly in simmering water. Drain tomatoes and let cool. Most cookbooks say to immerse the tomatoes in ice water right after draining, but I often skip this and just let the tomatoes sit. It's fine. While the tomatoes are cooling, chop or mince the onion and garlic. Fill a large pot with water for the pasta and set to boil.

Peel tomatoes, discarding the skins. Remove most of the seeds, but no need to be too meticulous about this. Chop tomatoes and reserve in a separate bowl. All of these steps so far may seem kind of a pain but they're worth it.

Heat a pan or skillet for the sauce. Add olive oil and butter. After the butter has melted, sauté onion. Add garlic. Don't let the garlic brown. Add the chopped tomatoes; it's fine to include any liquid that's accumulated. Add salt and a bit of pepper. Stir and sauté. Add white wine and simmer. Add more salt, to taste. Add a bit more wine, if you want. Let the sauce simmer and reduce, stirring occasionally, which may take anywhere from a few minutes to 10 minutes or more. Don't rush: it is *crucial* to let the sauce reduce.

During all of that time, cook the spaghetti, making sure it doesn't overcook. Drain pasta and add it to the sauce in the pan but not all at once so you can figure out your ideal proportion of sauce to pasta.

Serve in a large, pretty bowl—I swear this adds to the enjoyment of the food. Sprinkle optional basil or parsley on top and/or add freshly grated Parmigiano-Reggiano.

Eat while reading a good book.

THE BOUDIN TRAIL

NATALIE BASZILE

Natalie Baszile is the author of the debut novel *Queen Sugar*, which is being adapted for TV by writer-director Ava DuVernay and coproduced by Oprah Winfrey for OWN, Winfrey's cable network. *Queen Sugar* was named one of the *San Francisco Chronicle*'s Best Books of 2014 and nominated for an NAACP Image Award. Natalie has an MA in Afro-American studies from UCLA and holds an MFA from Warren Wilson College's MFA Program for Writers. Her nonfiction work has appeared in *The Rumpus*, *Lenny Letter*, *The Best Women's Travel Writing*, and *O, The Oprah Magazine*. She lives in the Bay Area.

It's two o'clock, a Thursday afternoon in early May, and the air inside the New Orleans airport smells like fried shrimp, mildew, and a hint of the Gulf. It's a comforting smell, at least to me, and every time I come in from California for a visit, the first thing I do stepping off the plane into the terminal is inhale deeply.

This trip, though, is different: I'm on a mission. I'm meeting my mother, my dad, and my sister, Jennifer, to whom I just started talking after a two-year estrangement.

Jennifer's flight from Connecticut is scheduled to arrive twenty minutes after mine. We've agreed to meet in baggage claim. The carousel has just lurched to life and suitcases are sliding down the black conveyor belt when I spot Jennifer at the top of the escalator. I can't help but stare. Even in jeans and a v-neck T-shirt, she looks downright regal.

Watching her descend, I try not to tense up. Long ago, I claimed Louisiana as mine and I'm still not eager to share it. I cringe at the thought of having to show my mom and sister around, taking them to the restaurants and shops I frequent, the out-of-the-way spots most tourists know nothing about. I'm being selfish, I know. If my Louisiana friends had been this closed-hearted with me, I'd still be a tourist, wandering down Bourbon Street with a fishbowl filled with green alcohol hanging from a cord around my neck.

Besides, my dad is the person I should really thank for introducing me to Louisiana. He was born and raised in Elton, a tiny town 190 miles to the west. And even though he hated almost everything about his life down here—hated the humidity and the grass growing up between cracks in the sidewalks; hated how every man in his family was pastor of a storefront church; hated Louisiana so much that he left the night of his high school graduation, set out for California and never looked back—he returned every spring to take his mother on a road trip. Grand Isle, Holly Beach, Natchitoches. Any place they could get to and back from in four days—which was all the time he could stand before he started remembering why he left in the first place.

When I was in college, he invited me to tag along, and even after my grandmother died, I kept coming back. From the first moment, I loved the heat and the crumbling buildings overtaken by kudzu. I loved the endless hours my aunts, uncles, and cousins spent in church. I loved Louisiana's earthiness, her accents and her twisting bayous. I loved it all—or mostly all. Jennifer joined us once or twice, but she never felt the same pull or burning passion. She was drawn to our mother's side of the family up in Detroit and was happy to leave Louisiana to me.

Come on, Baszile, I tell myself, *lighten up. This will be fun.* By the time Jennifer steps off the escalator, I'm feeling almost generous.

"Hey, Wench," I say, and hug her.

"Hey, Wench," Jen says, hugging me back.

This is our standard, sisterly hello, the way we've greeted each other since we were teenagers. But we haven't used the greeting at all lately and I can tell Jen is as nervous and relieved as I am to say the words. We used to be close. Used to call each other every day, sometimes *two or three times* a day, and then suddenly, two years ago, we stopped speaking. At the time, I was struggling to write my novel, going to grad school, and raising kids. Jennifer was divorcing her husband, writing a memoir, and leaving her university job. I don't remember the details of the argument, only that one day, neither of us picked up the phone. Days stretched into weeks. Weeks stretched into months. We didn't speak when her book was published or when my oldest daughter delivered her middle school graduation speech. We didn't speak when my dad's cancer came back a second time.

It was only after my dad landed in the hospital with failing kidneys that we finally reconciled. *It would be a shame if you two reconciled over your father's deathbed.* That's what my husband told Jen when he called to intervene. She called me a couple days later to say she was coming to San Francisco for a conference. She asked if we could meet. I drove to her hotel near the airport and saw her through the plate glass windows in the lobby. Before I could park, she was outside, standing beside my car.

An hour later, back in New Orleans, my mother arrives dressed in pleated pastel slacks and white patent loafers, a black quilted carry-on slung over her shoulder. She greets us with her signature beauty-contestant wave and flashes a toothy smile.

"Here they are," she says, standing on her toes to kiss us. "My two girls." She runs her hands through Jennifer's dreads, fingering the tiny cowry shell dangling from one of them.

"Where's Dad?" I ask.

Jennifer messages her temples.

Her tone is somber. "I can't believe we're doing this."

"Got him right here," Mom says, and she pats her carry-on conspiratorially.

A TRIP ALONG THE BOUDIN TRAIL was my idea. Three years ago, a friend sent me an article listing all the boudin—the mix of seasoned pork, beef, or crawfish and rice all stuffed into a sausage casing—in South Louisiana. The article linked to a website showing every grocery store, restaurant, gas station, and roadside stand along the two-hundred-mile strip between New Orleans and Lake Charles. If you planned right and had the stomach for it, the article said, you could hit every establishment in a single weekend, three days tops. The moment I finished the article, I called my dad.

"How'd you like to take a trip along the Boudin Trail?" I asked.

My dad was into slow food and "nose-to-tail eating" decades before the lifestyle became fashionable and trendy. *Black folks practically invented*

slow food, he liked to say. As a kid growing up in South Louisiana, he hunted raccoons, possums, and squirrels in the woods behind his house, then brought them home to his mother, who cooked them in stews. Sometimes, he shot an animal just to see how it tasted. Once, he shot and ate a crow.

"Let's do it," he said. "I'd like to get home one last time anyway." He'd just been diagnosed with leiomyosarcoma for the second time.

Instead, he spent most of the next two and a half years cycling through hospitals and rehab centers, growing frailer every month. Until the cancer, he'd never spent a night in a hospital, never broken a bone. By the end, he couldn't walk from the family room to the kitchen, couldn't hold a fork.

Now, it's just the three of us: my mother, Jen, and me. Mom transferred some of Dad's ashes from the urn she has at home into a small wooden container no bigger than a pack of cigarettes. That container is now safely zipped in a plastic Ziploc sandwich bag.

IN THE PARKING LOT, WE'VE JUST tossed our suitcases in the trunk when Jennifer notices my food bags—two oversized, insulated empty totes with heavy-duty zippers and straps wide as seatbelts.

"You've got to be kidding," she says.

"What?" I sound defensive. "Someone has to do it."

Dad always brought his food bags on our road trips so he could stock up. He bought boudin but also crawfish and the andouille sausage he used in his gumbo. By the time he purchased what he needed, we could barely zip the bags, each of which—between the food and the ice packs—weighed nearly fifty pounds. Dad treated his food bags like they were his children. He requested hotel rooms closest to the ice machine, monitored the bags' internal temperature to make sure the contents stayed cold, and carried them on the plane rather than check them as luggage.

Jennifer looks at me skeptically.

"Do you even know how to cook gumbo?"

"That's not the point." I fold the food bags and tuck them in among the suitcases.

WE'RE HURTLING DOWN I-10 when we spot Don's Specialty Meats, our first stop along the trail. Don's used to have a single location off Highway 49 in Carencro. Recently, they built a huge operation in Scott, just off the interstate frontage road. The building looks more like a casino with its enormous neon red sign and sprawling parking lot. We pull between two monster trucks.

Mom takes the Ziploc bag out of her carry-on.

How *do* you sprinkle someone's ashes in a store without alarming the proprietors or the customers? The question hasn't occurred to us until just now. We step inside Don's and feel the rush of air-conditioned air against our skin. The place is packed. There's a long line of people at the counter ordering boudin to go; another dozen shoppers plunder the deep freezers and banks of re-frigerators along the wall. I see no way to do this without someone noticing. And suddenly, all I can think of are the sanitation laws we're surely breaking. I'm about to chicken out when mom comes up behind me gripping a plastic spoon.

"I got this from the girl at the counter." She grins.

Jennifer posts herself near the front counter and keeps watch while mom and I wander to the back corner. Mom opens the Zip-loc, lifts the lid off the wooden box, and scoops out a quarter teaspoon of what looks like tiny bits of gravel and grit. She bends low and sprinkles the cremains of my father under the last refrigerator, back far enough that no one will notice. They look pale and gray, almost like silt, against the dirty white floor tiles.

I've never seen Dad's ashes before. I think back on all the years I heard Mom scold Dad for being overweight; how he loved to walk barefoot through the garden we planted behind my house because the feel of his feet in the soil reminded him of his Louisiana childhood—and my mind can't compute. I can't reconcile those memories with the spoonful of dust.

Mom dips the white spoon into the bag again, then looks at me. "I think we should say something."

Her suggestion catches me flat-footed. Until now, the tone of our trip has been easy and lighthearted. We've cracked off-color jokes and reminisced about the time Dad glided right off the treadmill and broke his arm. We shake our heads in wonder at the time he took twelve Aleve tablets in one sitting. It's gallows humor, we know, but it's our way of coping. *Why are we getting serious now?* I wonder. Besides, Jennifer's the better public speaker. Three years my junior, she has al-ways possessed a seriousness, an intensity that makes most people assume she's older. She delivered the eulogy at Dad's memorial that had everyone in tears.

"Well, Dad," I say, fumbling for words. "I guess this is it."

As the refrigerators hum behind me, I think about how, before he got sick, people often mistook him for Muhammad Ali. It was easy to do. He had the presence and personality to match. If he were here now, he'd be sauntering down the aisles, his arms loaded with frozen packages of smoked boudin and andouille sausage, never bothering to disabuse staring onlookers of their belief he might be the real prizefighter. Now, standing under the fluorescent lights in the bustling store, I thank Dad aloud for letting me tag along on all those road trips. I tell him about my book. I tell him Mom's going to be okay and that Jennifer and I are talking again.

When I finish, Mom grabs my hand and squeezes.

We give Jennifer the signal—two thumbs up—and the three of us walk back to the car.

Two more stops along the trail and we've established a rhythm to scattering ashes. The Best Stop Supermarket. Billy's Boudin &

Cracklins. My mother keeps the plastic spoon. We have our good-byes down to five minutes. We pass through Saint Martinville and sprinkle cremains in the parking lot of Joyce's Supermarket. Rabideaux's in Iowa doesn't sell boudin, but we swing by anyway because Dad swore they made the best andouille in South Louisiana. It's a tiny shop with a counter and a single display case. To keep from getting busted, we mix ashes into the soil of a potted palm near the door.

The Walmart Supercenter in Jennings is our last stop before we call it quits for the night. The place is larger than three football fields and it takes us a while to find the Outdoor/Sportsman section, which is where the insulated food bags are sold. As far as Dad was concerned, you couldn't have too many. We pick out one we think he would have liked—navy blue with tan handles as wide as our hands—and place it on the bottom shelf. Then scoop out a heaping spoonful of cremains and sprinkle them liberally underneath. The cleaning crew will mop this aisle by this time tomorrow. At least we've paid our respects.

The next morning we drive to Elton, Dad's hometown. When Dad was a kid, he planted an oak sapling in his front yard. The house he grew up in has long since been razed, but the sapling is now a massive oak tree—four stories tall with roots so thick they've buckled the sidewalk.

Here is a scene: Two sisters stand at the base of an enormous oak—a tree their dad planted sixty-five years earlier. They are surrounded by twenty-five people—aunts and uncles and cousins; their great aunt Dell, who just turned ninety-three; and a few of their father's childhood friends. Their cousin, Antoinette, steps forward and sings the first verse of "At the Cross"—their dad's favorite hymn. Her voice is crisp and clear. A siren's voice that rises into the oak tree's highest branches. And when the rest of the crowd joins in the singing, the sound carries down the street and out to the road. The group sings two more hymns, both a cappella, the way black folks in the south used to sing when the girls' dad was a boy. The moment has an old-timey feel.

When the singing stops, the sisters hold hands. They watch their Uncle Sonny dig a hole between the tree roots. Their mother places the little wooden box inside, and then their Uncle Charles fills the hole with concrete and places a small marble headstone over the spot.

It's done. Their dad is home.

IT'S A LONG DRIVE BACK TO NEW Orleans. Jennifer and I are speaking again, a gift of my father's illness—but no one has much to say. We pass all the boudin joints we visited along the way, but this time, we don't stop. I don't realize how different, how sacred, a trip this has been from what I expected till I get to the airport and see them again: my food bags.

They are empty.

Boudin Sausage

2 quarts water

2 pounds pork (this is
   traditional, but you can
   also use beef, duck—
   whatever you prefer),
   cut into 1-inch cubes

½ pound pork or chicken
   livers

1 medium yellow onion,
   chopped

4 cloves garlic, minced

1 green bell pepper,
   seeded and chopped

1 celery rib, diced

1 tablespoon kosher salt,
   divided

2 ½ teaspoons cayenne,
   divided

1 teaspoon black pepper,
   divided

1 cup parsley, finely chopped

2 cups green onions, chopped
   (green part only)

2 cups cooked rice

1 ½-inch diameter casings,
   about 4 feet in length

Add 2 quarts water to a large saucepan, then add the pork, livers, yellow onion, garlic, bell pepper, celery, 1 teaspoon salt, ¼ teaspoon cayenne, and ¼ teaspoon black pepper. Bring the water to a boil and then reduce it to a simmer uncovered for about an hour and a half, until the pork and liver are tender. Remove from the heat and strain the meat and vegetables, reserving 1 ½ cups of the broth. Finely dice the meat, vegetables, ½ cup of the parsley, and ½ cup of the green onions (you can also do this in a food processor or meat grinder).

Once it's been diced, place the mixture into a mixing bowl. Add the cooked rice and the remaining salt, cayenne, black pepper, parsley, and green onions. Then add the reserved broth, ½ cup at a time, and mix well until the filling is cohesive and slightly sticky. Stuff the filling into sausage casings, making 3-inch links. Either grill the sausage or bring one gallon of salted water close to a boil (steaming hot but not bubbling) and poach the sausage links for about 5 to 10 minutes, until firm. Serve.

ACKNOWLEDGMENTS

S o many people poured love into this book. For their kindness and generosity, my heartfelt gratitude goes to: my amazing, unwavering agent, Jody Kahn, for her astute advice, sensitivity, and friendship; my editor Leigh Newman, for her keen eye, enthusiasm, and indispensable wisdom; my publisher, Andy Hunter, and the entire team at Black Balloon/ Catapult—Wah-Ming Chang, Alisha Gorder, Megan Fishmann, Elizabeth Ireland, Nicole Caputo, and more—for giving this book such a good home; illustrator Meryl Rowin, for making the book glow. I'm lucky to work with all of you.

Thank you to beloved pals Edith Zimmerman, Amy Jean Porter, and Elisabeth Waterston for sustaining me with big hearts, wild imaginations, and overall wonderfulness. And thank you to my family, especially my parents, for years of delicious inspiration.

I'm unendingly grateful for and indebted to the thirty-one authors who contributed to *Eat Joy*. Thank you for trusting me with your stories. Your words mean more to me than you could ever know.

Finally, thank you to Tony, Serafina, and Aurelio, for everything. You are forever the source of my joy.

PERMISSIONS

Grateful acknowledgement is made to the following for permission to reprint previously published materials:

"Sierra Leone, 1997" by Chimamanda Ngozi Adichie, originally published in *The New Yorker*. Copyright © 2006 Chimamanda Ngozi Adichie. Used by permission of The Wylie Agency LLC.

"The Boudin Trail" by Natalie Baszile, adapted from an earlier version that was first published in *Better Than Fiction 2* (Lonely Planet, 2015). Copyright © 2015 by Natalie Baszile. Used by permission of the author.

"Cleanse" by Alexander Chee was first published on *The Morning News* in October 2013. The recipe is adapted from an earlier version that was first published in *Stock Tips: A Zine About Soup* (2014). Copyright © 2013 by Alexander Chee. Used by permission of the author.

"A Grain of Comfort" by Edwidge Danticat was first published in the April 2006 issue of *O, The Oprah Magazine*. Copyright © 2006 by Edwidge Danticat. Used by permission of the author and Aragi Inc.

"Homesick at the Outer Edge of the World" by Anthony Doerr, adapted from an earlier version that was first published in the January 2014 issue of *1843*. Copyright © 2014 by Anthony Doerr. Used by permission of the author.

NATALIE EVE GARRETT is an artist and writer, and the editor of *The Artists' and Writers' Cookbook: A Collection of Stories with Recipes.* She lives in a town outside Washington, D.C., along the Potomac River with her husband and two children.